The Changing Family

Views from Theology and the Social Sciences
in the Light of the Apostolic Exhortation
Familiaris Consortio

Edited by Stanley L. Saxton
Patricia Voydanoff
Angela Ann Zukowski, M.H.S.H.

A Campion Book

Loyola University Press
Chicago 60657

Quotations from the text of *On the Family*, Apostolic Exhortation *Familiaris Consortio*, copyright © 1982, United States Catholic Conference, Washington, D.C. Used with permission.

LIBRARY OF CONGRESS CATALOGING IN PUBLICATION DATA

Main entry under title:

The Changing Family.

Papers from a symposium organized by the University of Dayton.
    1. Family—Religious life—Congresses. 2. Family—Congresses. 3. Sex role—Congresses. 4. Catholic Church—Doctrines—Congresses. I. Voydanoff, Patricia II. University of Dayton.
BX2351.C48 1984   261.8'3585   84-7924
ISBN 0-8294-0458-9

CONTENTS

PREFACE

The University of Dayton's National Symposium on *Familiaris Consortio* took place because of the vision and support of Brother Raymond L. Fitz, S. M., Ph.D., President of the University of Dayton. His commitment to the welfare of families led him to see the value of a symposium that would explore the implications of *Familiaris Consortio* for the quality of family life. Brother Leonard Mann, S. M., Dean of the College of Arts and Sciences, and Most Reverend Joseph L. Bernardin, then Archbishop of Cincinnati, assisted in the early planning of the symposium. Dr. Francis M. Lazarus, Dean of the College of Arts and Sciences, participated in the later planning and the execution of the symposium.

The symposium committee of the Center for the Study of Family Development had anticipated that *Familiaris Consortio* would appear in print early in 1981, but the assassination attempt upon the life of Pope John Paul II delayed publication of the document until December 1981. After receiving the official text of the exhortation, the committee was able to make final decisions about pariticpants and topics of the papers.

Not until we had read *Familiaris Consortio* in final form did the symposium committee fully understand and appreciate the problems that social scientists might have in analyzing an official church document. Most social scientists are trained in empirical methodologies and their respective disciplines are dominated by an epistemology that calls for the pursuit of knowledge through the use of systematic empirical investigation. This is not to say that all social scientists are empiricists. There are those who choose instead to organize their research around qualitative methodologies addressing issues of humanistic or critical interpretive concerns.

The epistemology of *Familiaris Consortio* is consistent with a long and rich tradition of Catholic theological dogma. The statement clearly and elegantly expresses a vision of family consistent with church teachings. The question the CSFD symposium committee faced was: "In what manner is the epistemology of the social sciences consistent with, or contradictory to, the epistemology of dogmatic tradition?" Can social scientists who maintain fidelity to their "way of knowing" meaningfully deal with church statements that are true to a pastoral or ecclesiastical method of knowing about the human condition? To quote *Familiaris Consortio*:

> The church values sociological and statistical research when it proves helpful in understanding the historical context in which pastoral action has to be developed and when it leads to a better understanding of the truth. Such research alone, however, is not to be considered in itself an expression of the sense of faith (FC§5).

For most social scientists the position expressed in this quote is entirely acceptable. For example, sociological information should help clarify historical contexts, and sociological scientific research rarely makes claims of truth per se. Furthermore, it is not necessary that sociological research intrude upon, or perhaps even be directly relevant to, beliefs based upon faith. Sociological theory may offer alternative explanations for behavior that is of interest to the church; for example, church attendance. Sociological and faith-based explanations are, however, rarely in competition with one another. For the most part, they coexist in separate domains of discussion, usually without tension or conflict. This understanding of their separate domains and functions—the church as the body of faith and sociology as the science of society—does not, however, eliminate the communication problems. When these domains overlap because of intersecting interests and consequences, communication will most likely be lively and interesting but also most likely will be tense and conflictual.

Concern for, and study of, the family is an area where interests of the church and sociological analysis overlap. Both the church and the discipline of sociology have traditionally studied the family, and both have produced scholarly writings based on their findings. The CSFD symposium committee was faced with the challenge of selecting a group of family scholars who could prepare papers whch focused upon selected topics covered in *Familiaris Consortio*. In turn, these scholars were faced with the challenge of negotiating a path between two different epistemologies in a manner that made it possible for them to be faithful to their own epistemology and respectful of the other. The committee solved this issue by choosing theologians and religious studies scholars who were sensitive to, and interested in, social science literature; and by choosing social scientists who were knowledgeable about, and sensitive to, traditions of thought in the church. Consequently, we believe a unique group of scholars was brought together to focus on the topic of the family. The meaningful, informal discussion between the theologians and social scientists that occurred during the symposium is reflected in the papers of this volume. It is our impression that the theologians who participated in the symposium were as willing to grapple with sociological and economic data and theory as the social scientists were willing to delve into the realm of theological discourse. This symposium report illustrates the kind of results that are possible when members of the theological and social science communities are willing to work together on a mutually relevant topic of inquiry, proving that each domain of study can inform the other, even though formidable epistemological boundaries exist.

After the symposium, the following University of Dayton faculty assisted in the preparation of the manuscript by reviewing the papers and suggesting revisions: Judith P. Allik, Eugene R. August, Berthold Berg, Rita J. Bowen, Brenda W. Donnelly, Rev. Robert J. Hater, Rev. James L. Heft, S. M., Linda C. Majka, Thomas M. Martin, Roger D. McCormick, Stephen J. McNamee, and Sandra Moore.

We wish to express our appreciation to all these people, who made this book possible. We are especially grateful to the symposium participants whose thoughtful contributions form the substance of the book.

STANLEY L. SAXTON
PATRICIA VOYDANOFF
ANGELA ANN ZUKOWSKI, M.H.S.H.

Center for the Study of Family Development
The University of Dayton
Dayton, Ohio

Introduction

David M. Thomas, Ph.D.

THE ROLE OF VATICAN SYNODS

The experience of Vatican II stimulated the appetite of the Church for further conversations and processes which would build upon the gains already achieved. The proposal was made, therefore, to hold regularly scheduled international meetings of church leadership with the Holy Father to discuss and deal with significant issues of church life. Two years after the conclusion of Vatican II the first of these synods was convened with no less than five major items set for discussion and deliberation. The task of adequately dealing with such a range of topics proved insurmountable, and over the years the synod format has been reduced to the discussion of a single topic. In 1980, the topic needing attention and a fitting pastoral response by the Church was the family.

What follows are my personal reflections on both what went on in Rome during the month of October 1980 and my judgment concerning the positive and negative aspects of this particular meeting. My role was that of an official advisor *(peritus)* to the United States bishops delegation. I played no formal role within the synod itself, although the advisory staff of our bishops worked closely with our official delegates in formulating the various interventions given to the synod body.

An understanding of the synod, itself, is necessary for gaining a full understanding of *Familiaris Consortio* because it is part of a response to a conversation, the first part being the synod deliberations and formal resolutions given to the Holy Father at the conclusion of the synod. If one only knows one side of a conversation there is always the danger of missing a significant phrase or a meaningful response.

In discussing a synod, one immediately encounters a difficulty relating to the role of synods in official church teaching. Vatican II restored in church thinking a strong sense of the total church and its role, particularly through its bishops, in formulating church thought. In a sense the Roman Catholic bishops of the world came of age during the meetings of Vatican II. Their words were respected; their ideas became building blocks for a new view of church and society. It was expected by some that the synod format would continue this process of effective and significant involvement on the part of the bishops themselves in formulating new advances in church life, particularly in the area of responding to pastoral needs of individuals both inside and outside the church. Yet this sense of healthy autonomy was never allowed to reach full stature because the synod deliberations were consistently viewed as simply advisory to the pope. This principle has been stated quite clearly in the recently promulgated Revised Code of Canon Law.

The advisory role of the synod was taken quite seriously by the pope as he faithfully attended every synodal meeting and listened with attention and concentration. Furthermore, the delegates themselves exhibited a strong freedom of expression which meant that individual bishops were not afraid to call into question traditional doctrinal and pastoral positions, nor were they afraid to challenge their peers. A variety of languages was allowed, along with many forms of expression. Delegates cited formal church teachings. They recounted the family situations in their own countries. They told stories about their own families. They used parable and poetry along with sometimes biting prose to communicate their concern and interest. The input was generally rich and worthwhile, although one sometimes wondered whether anything would come from all that was offered. It was possible for the Holy Father to ignore some or all of what was said, although it has to be added that he did not do this.

THE REPRESENTATIVE NATURE OF THE SYNOD

Over two hundred bishops from virtually every corner of the world were present. A small number of superiors from religious communities were also involved. But most significant, I feel, were the laity who were invited to sit with the delegates during the actual synod sessions. It is noteworthy that the invitation to these *auditores* (listeners), as they were called, came at the last minute and apparently from the explicit wish of the pope himself. Numbering about thirty, they, too, were drawn from all the continents of the world, most of them being married couples. A disproportionate number of them represented the formal interests of the Natural Family Planning Movement, which resulted in a feeling that this concern was, perhaps, the major concern of the laity. This is not to call into question their presence, nor their interests, but only to note that a sense of the laity might have been different if there had been a broader representation of views and interests.

During the first two weeks of the synod itself, the auditores played their listening role quite well; they were not allowed to address the synod body. A concern about this restriction was first expressed by the bishop delegates themselves, who mentioned often that the laity should not only listen but also have a formal voice in the synod deliberations. The Secretariat for the synod, not having planned for these interventions, did not appear to be pleased at revising the meeting format to include the laity. However, after it became clear that most of the bishops desired to hear from the laity, two couples were notified that they would be allowed to address the synod. Eventually this would be viewed by some of the bishops as tokenism and in the end all the auditores were allowed time to address the synod. This was viewed by many as a major breakthrough in formal church discussions, symbolizing at least the rightful role of the laity in expressing their faith and their experience in areas of life with which they are most familiar. When the delegates divided into small language groups for more informal sharing, the laity were allowed a full voice.

Another notable feature of the representative character of the synod was the large number of delegates from the Third World countries. One of the largest delegations, for instance, was from Africa, and their presence was quite influential in shaping the discussion of family life in non-Western countries. Because of the diversity of delegates, some wondered whether any document or single response to the synod could in any way adequately respect the diversity present at the meeting. In interpreting *Familiaris Consortio,* what must be kept in mind is that the pope attempted in his exhortation to respond to Third World concerns, which often focus on the very survival of the family, as well as to respond to First World concerns, which focus on such issues as intimacy, divorce, and birth regulation.

SYNOD PREPARATION

Each country went through a different procedure in preparing for the synod. Both Canada and England used national pastoral hearings as a basis for the content of their interventions. The United States delegates worked with local family life personnel and sought assistance from the theological community. In the summer before the synod a major symposium was held at the University of Notre Dame, which brought together the synod delegates from Canada and the United States in a meeting shared with representatives from both the pastoral side and the academic side of the church.

Based on this meeting and on work with their consultors, the United States bishops formulated various interventions before they actually went to Rome. Most of these were revised in light of developments within the synod itself and strengthened by further work between the delegates and their advisors.

A few months before the synod, the Secretariat for the synod (a Vatican office) published a document outlining a suggested format for the meeting. It was feared by some that the work of the synod itself would merely be *pro forma* based on the fact that Rome had already decided those things that should come from the synod. In actual fact, however, this preliminary document merely stimulated discussion and reaction, and was set aside as soon as the synod began.

THE SYNOD PROCESS

The synod began with each delegate being allowed a short period of time, usually eight minutes, to speak to an issue of the synod in whatever way he wished to do so. Initially, presentations were made in Latin, although it became apparent in the first few days of the meeting that this requirement seriously hampered free expression. It was therefore decided that each delegate could speak in his own language with simultaneous translation provided to the other delegates. Because each delegate was scheduled to speak simply in the order in which he made his request, the deliberations in the first two weeks tended to be disconnected. There was little sense of development, although certain themes emerged. It was abundantly clear that each delegate cared deeply about the family and had the hope that the church would issue practical pastoral responses to the needs of the Christian family. As honorable as this attitude was, it also betrayed a sense of separation between the church and the family itself. Little was said, for example, about the way in which the family is the church, a special embodiment of the local Christian community. Much was said about what the church might do for the family; little was said about the family's contribution to church life. As the laity were allowed more of a voice within the synod, this participation began to change the thinking of some of the bishops and they began to *learn* from the laity. Unfortunately, this insight was late in coming and too weak in expression to play a major role in the final resolutions of the synod.

From my own point of view, the greatest disappointment was the lack of a serious consideration of the theology of the family. When synodal discussion focused on the theological topic, it was clear that the delegates were only able to repeat traditional formulae and not engage in thought that might advance earlier theological formulations. In general, the propositions of earlier church documents were repeated, neither calling into question their adequacy in the present order, nor attempting to advance promising insights—even those of Vatican II. This lack of theological development is also evidenced in the pope's response in *Familiaris Consortio*. It is difficult to determine whether this lack of development was caused by the delegates' lack of theological expertise, or their general unwillingness to move beyond past formulations. There was open opposition to any questioning of past formulations. This was done by representatives of the Curia who, while not in the majority, nevertheless maintained a signficant vocal presence during the deliberations. While the Holy Father remained silent throughout the synod, he did use the closing ceremony to restate traditional approaches to such issues as the reception of the Eucharist by remarried Catholics. Part of the reason for the lack of any sustained theological discussion was the synod format itself, which neither encouraged nor facilitated any development of thought. The agenda was left to the delegates themselves, and with two to three hundred participants it was virtually impossible to keep on a particular topic. Many bishops urgently called for a new theology of the family, of marriage, and of sexuality; but none seemed prepared to articulate these new theologies. Final synod resolutions recommended the creation of an international body of bishops, laity, and theologians to explore these areas. But at least for now, no effort has been made on the part of the Vatican to initiate this discussion.

The synod was scheduled to last about five weeks. In the fourth week of the meeting, an attempt was made by a special subcommittee of the synod under the direction of Cardinal Ratzinger to formulate a set of resolutions that would summarize and synthesize the combined thought of the delegates. This group's summary was offered to a select committee of bishops from the various language groups for approval. After reviewing the Ratzinger summary, the bishops were compelled to reject the summary, noting particularly its lack of theological sensitivity. This put the synod in something of a crisis because the goal was to formulate a set of propositions after careful discussion and debate. In fact, what was needed was a quick organization of small working groups, each of which was assigned an area to develop new resolutions. Once these new resolutions were formulated, they were submitted to the total body of the synod, at which time they were debated and revised, and then finally put to a vote. It was these resolutions which were given to John Paul II at the conclusion of the synod.

After reading the resolutions and comparing them with the final wording of *Familiaris Consortio*, my own judgment is that the pope was quite faithful to both the spirit and the letter of the resolutions. He attempted to capture their pastoral concern for the family, while at the same time he did not attempt to move beyond the theological and cultural diversity present among the synod delegates. This fact renders the pope's document more of what I would call "a scissors and paste product" rather than the expression of a single author. In this sense the pope seems to have acted more as a synthesizer, or translator, of the mind of the synod than as a creative author attempting to advance church thought on family life. Nor does there seem to be any evidence that the pope expressed many of his own ideas on sexuality and marriage. For example, there is little reference to his lengthy discussions of the theology of sexuality which were given at his Wednesday audiences both before, during, and after the synod.

Conclusion

Synods provide a unique opportunity for the church leadership to participate in a conversation about significant issues. The careful way delegates are chosen from the national episcopal conferences and the preparation of these delegates could very well establish a privileged moment for church development. The concept of regular synodal meetings is a good one, for not only can a synod provide an opportunity to focus on an issue but it can also be the means by which new perceptions are reached. This was true of the synod on justice in 1971 and of the synod on evangelization in 1974. The fact that a synod was to focus on the role of the Christian family in 1980 was good reason, therefore, to have increased hope for families around the world. While the gifts and problems of families vary from region to region, nevertheless, all families experience in some way the living Spirit of God in their midst. A review of the synodal discussion suggests that a sincere sense of sympathy exists in the church for the trials now experienced by families everywhere. One can conclude that the church cares deeply about helping families. Yet, one can question whether the church can adequately assist families if it does not consider the place of families to be at the very center of church life. One can also question how a discussion about family life that does not involve the laity can ever produce significant and satisfactory results from both a human and a Christian perspective. In defense of the Holy Father, and with respect for the deep concern expressed by most of the bishop delegates to the synod, I feel that they would agree with this principle of lay and family involvement in discussing the topics that surfaced at the synod. But in many ways the official church is a victim of its history, and this history has not valued such input. An attempt was made to break this tradition by inviting and eventually involving laity within the synod processes. Yet, it would also have to be said that this was *only* a beginning. Time will tell whether the church is really serious about creating new formats for advancing its official teachings. Many of the bishops appeared dissatisfied with their role as mere advisors to the pope. Vatican II spoke of collegiality and the role of the bishops as interpreters of God's Word. This same council also spoke about the competency of the laity to discuss matters that directly touch their lives. There were moments during the synod when this was both allowed and encouraged. But the result was often imperfect and undeveloped. However, this shortcoming should not be taken in any way as a reason for discontinuing this process.

Behind the words of the synod and *Familiaris Consortio* there exists a strong sentiment that the future of the church and society rests upon, and relates to, the life of the Christian family. A few bishops were heard to say that the institutional church should make an effort to develop the ideas sometimes only hinted at during the synod. They had a sense that more time was needed for discussion, reflection, and formulation. What this means in practice, I believe, is a need for another synod on a topic directly related to that of the synod of 1980. Given the continued importance of the topic and its practical impact in every land where Christians live, it seems imperative that both formal and informal discussion continue. Many of the resolutions of the synod spoke to this need for further dialog. This is picked up in *Familiaris Consortio* and applied primarily to the local level. And although local discussion is needed, so is a discussion at the highest level of church life, because the issues surfaced at the synod affect the entire church. The announcement that the topic for the synod scheduled in 1986 will be the laity may provide an opportune moment for a return to topics of central interest to the laity—sexuality, marriage, and the family.

PART ONE

Theology of Marriage and the Family

Introduction

Reflecting changes in family life, the media over the past ten years have challenged our understanding of the nature of the family. As the family has gradually changed its functions in society, so the Catholic family has changed its relationship with the Church. It is for this reason that *Familiaris Consortio* is significant. The exhortation offers the Church and society an opportunity to reconsider the meaning, value, and place of the family in the parish and in the civic community. Yet, the exhortation says even more about our theology of what it means to be Church today. Identifying the family as "the domestic church" places the family in a unique relationship to the Church. "The Christian famiy, in fact, is the first community called to announce the Gospel to the human person during growth and to bring him or her, through a progressive education and catechesis, to full human and Christian maturity"(FC§2). This recognition of the family as a true and significant embodiment of the Church encourages the family to look not only without but within itself for strength and support in the growth and development of the religious life and the fostering of the Kingdom of God.

Maureen Gallagher emphasizes the sacramentality of the family. As sacrament, the family has the power to become a source and celebration of God's self-communication. To appreciate the family as sacrament is to begin to recognize, respect, and respond to the presence of God revealed in each and every family event. The ordinary becomes extraordinary. The simple everyday experiences of nourishing, forgiving, and affirming one another prepare us to understand and celebrate the sacramental rituals of the Church.

David Thomas continues Gallagher's theme by identifying spirituality as an important ingredient in the development of intimacy in the family. He sees spirituality as the meshing in daily life of a set of deep relationships. The relational life of the family involves a deep relationship with God who is experienced as a real, personal presence, active and living in the lives of each family member. How the family lives together in that divine presence is what constitutes family spirituality.

3

In the final article of this section, Michael Place analyzes the theological dimensions of the exhortation. He systematically compares views presented in *Familiaris Consortio* with those of several contemporary theologians on the topics of the meaning and sacramentality of Christian marriage, the significance of human sexuality, and responses to marital failure. The paper ends with a call for serious dialogue "in order that a consistent or integrated vision can be offered to the church."

1

Family as Sacrament

Maureen Gallagher

ARCHDIOCESE OF MILWAUKEE

Familiaris Consortio uses the word sacrament in the narrowly defined sense of seven sacraments. However, there are some theological under-pinnings in the document which allow us to develop a thesis that the family itself is a sacrament and that it celebrates its sacramentality within itself and within the larger Christian community.

Familiaris Consortio calls the laity to interpret temporal realities in the light of Christ and to offer their unique and irreplaceable authentic discernment to the larger church (FC§5). The document also refers to the rich understanding and full integration of the mystery of Christ in their lives (FC§9). The rich understanding that families can offer the larger church emerges from a self-understanding that they are indeed a fundamental sac-rament and they do indeed celebrate sacramentality within their experi-ence of family.

To develop this idea, I shall present an understanding of sacrament that is a framework for the thesis, examine family life in the light of their understanding of sacrament, and finally, examine the document to deter-mine how its theological understanding is congruent with the idea of family as sacrament.

SACRAMENTALITY

In creation the world is permeated by God's grace. The very core of the world is graced by God's presence. The celebration of this fact is the heart of sacramentality. Grace is not something the Church gives when one performs rituals correctly. Grace is a gift from God—God's self-commu-nication which is present whether it is accepted by people or not. Rahner points out:

> This grace is not a particular phenomenon occurring parallel to the rest of human life but simply the ultimate depth of everything the

5

spiritual creature does. When he realizes himself—when he laughs and cries, accepts responsibility, loves, lives, and dies, stands up for truth, breaks out of preoccupation with self to help the neighbor, hopes against hope, cheerfully refuses to be embittered by the stupidity of daily life, keeps silent not so that evil festers in his heart but so that it dies there—when in a word, man lives as he would like to live, in opposition to his selfishness and to the despair that always assails him. This is where grace occurs, because all this leads man into the infinity and victory that is God (Rahner, 1971).

Grace is most perfectly manifested in Jesus who lived his life of ordinariness (which is comparable to ours) in an extraordinary manner. Because he accepted the presence and love of God, he was able to see his life differently. He saw more than meets the eye. As Teilhard de Chardin writes: "By reason of creation and even more the incarnation, nothing is profane for those who know how to see." How did Jesus see his life? Jesus saw a purpose or meaning in the ordinary. This distinctive way of seeing made the ordinary extraordinary. This seeing was the recognition of God's presence, of ultimate meaning in ordinary events. Jesus not only was the incarnation of God in human life, he saw incarnation all around him. He took as his mission the initiation of others into the incarnational mysteries of God. He used parables to say "see differently"; He accented his words with visible signs of invisible reality.

We have described grace as the self-giving of God to the world and demonstrated that grace is epitomized in Jesus and his life of the ordinary made new by seeing anew. Another aspect of grace, which is at the heart of sacramentality, is the communal nature of grace. Because of the social nature of reality experienced by human beings, we cannot discuss grace only in relationship to individuals. Individuals always exist in relationship with others. Grace is interrelational insofar as individuals are in solidarity with the human race.

In order to understand Christian sacraments then, we need to include an awareness of Jesus' relationships to the community. Recognizing the specialness of their brother Jesus, the early disciples saw him as a person for God and about God. Their imagination was captured by the vision Jesus had of how things could be. After the death and resurrection of Jesus, the disciples wanted to pursue the vision he had of the Godliness of the world, which was their own graced existence. In a very real sense, the early Christians saw Jesus as the sacrament of encounter with God—the sign of God's Word and deed present in their everyday experience. God had graced their lives, given their lives a focus, a purpose, a reason for living—the greatest sign of this was Jesus himself.

The early Christians saw the presence of God's grace in Jesus and celebrated this first and foremost when they shared a meal together. There they recalled the presence of the Lord in their lives. They shared food and wine and recalled the events of Jesus' life. In doing this they evoked Jesus' very presence with them. They used their ordinary rituals and saw them in a new way.

The uniqueness of the Judeo-Christian faith lies in its experience and celebration of God's presence in life experiences. The biblical notion of faith always rooted faith in human experience. It was not an abstract, intellectual understanding of God's presence. Faith was seen as a force of life. People were rooted in faith. Grace was not a holy addition to life, but the core of life.

Sacraments grew out of the experiences of human life. Sacraments became events which the Christian community used to transform the ordinariness of human life, live it out in slow motion as a ritual, and in so doing come to a new realization of God's presence in the fabric of daily existence. The rituals that in the course of events became known as sacraments were not to make life automatically holy; rather, they pointed to the holiness which was inherent in a faith-filled existence and celebrated this awareness of inherent holiness communally.

Sacraments help people to be aware of the Godliness of life. They point to the extraordinary in the ordinary. They say there's "more than meets the eye" in birth, in death, in nurturing, in healing, in forgiving, in working through vocational pursuits, in growing through relationships, in helping one another cope with the realities of life.

The essential underlying theological concepts of sacramentality relate to: (1) God's self-communication with the world; (2) the recognition and acceptance of this in the ordinary events of life which is the task of faith; (3) the celebration of this grace within the community.

This concept of sacramentality is basic to any defined idea of Christian sacraments. Otherwise, Christian sacraments stand in danger of being understood in a way that borders on magic or in a manner that gives identity only to the clergy at the expense of the community.

FAMILY LIFE AND SACRAMENTALITY

We have established that one of the primary reasons for doing sacraments is to recognize and celebrate the holiness in daily experience. Where can we find the power of God? In the family. Where can we see the "more than meets the eye" dimension of human experience? In the family. Where do we see people coming together in search of a purpose for living? In the family.

Theologians consider Jesus the primary sacrament of God's encounter with humanity (Schillebeeckx, 1963). Jesus by word and action made God's presence and care known. Jesus is truly a sacrament. Taken from another aspect, the Church is considered a sacrament because the Church by word and action manifests God's presence and proclaims the God dimension interwoven in life's experiences. The family can also be considerd a sacrament. The family by word and deed manifests God's presence and leads its members to see the holiness which is part of everyday existence. For children, their primary experience of God is in their families. Whether in single parent or two parent families, children can know of God's care because they experience parental care; they can know of God's acceptance because they experience parental acceptance; they know of God's nurture because they know parental nurture; they can know of God's steadfastness because they experience parental steadfastness. The same is true of forgiveness, healing, and affirmation of many kinds.

Not only is God's presence made known to children through at least one parent, but children themselves become the signs of God to parents. Co-creation is of itself an experience of Godliness. It doesn't have to be explained, nor does it have to be the focus of theology. Birth can be an ecstatic experience, an experience of the transcendent.

Even if one were to isolate particular events in family life, one would find that many of these parallel what we know as the seven sacraments. For instance, a series of events initiate children into adulthood: from teaching a child how to tie shoes to how to drive a car, there is constant calling forth and affirmation by the family. In fact, family life is full of initiation rituals which say to the person "we love you" or "we're glad you're here." Not only do parents initiate children into adulthood, but children initiate parents into the various challenges of parenthood. Initiation, affirmation, and accomplishment rituals (such as birthday parties, mortgage burnings, rituals related to losing teeth, obtaining a driver's license, and making the team) in a real sense flesh out the baptism and confirmation celebrated by the larger community. Family rituals such as these are family sacraments if they are recognized for their inherent value and seen in relationship to growth and development in Christian faith.

Nurturing is another basic ingredient of famiy life which is sacramental. Nurturing is seen on many levels: physical, psychological, emotional, and spiritual. One needs to be nurtured well at home before one can understand the community's celebration of Eucharist. Nurturing at home is in a real sensé First Eucharist. The community of the family is the first sign of God's nourishment. Parents provide the first sacramental celebrations when they help children to see the "more than" just tangible food which makes up family meals.

Healing and forgiveness are also part of the "weft and warp" of family existence. Brokenness is often first experienced in family relationships. Reconciliation binds families together and helps them grow in relationships which affect the larger community.

Without belaboring this, we have pointed to the inherent holiness in family life and its sacramental celebration in the daily life of families. So, then, to return to the claim made at the beginning of this paper, does *Familiaris Consortio* allow for such an interpretation of the sacramentality of family life?

FAMILIARIS CONSORTIO

The theology of sacramentality and family life which has been highlighted above is implicit in the theology which underlies *Familiaris Consortio*. I state this for the following reasons:

First: the theology of grace which underlies sacramental theology as described by Rahner earlier in the paper ("When a person laughs, cries, accepts responsibility, loves, lives...this is where grace occurs") is congruent with a theology of grace implicit in the document. An example of this is seen in relationship to grace and the building of the family community.

All members of the family, each according to his or her own gift, have the grace and responsibility of building day by day the communion of persons, making the family "a school of deeper humanity": This happens where there is care and love for the little ones, the sick, the aged; where there is mutual service every day; when there is sharing of goods, of joys and of sorrows (FC§21).

Furthermore, the document quoting Paul VI states that within a family "all members evangelize and are evangelized" (FC§ 39). Quoting the Second Vatican Council, *Familiaris Consortio* says that "By virtue of this sacrament [marriage], as spouses fulfill their conjugal and family obligations they are penetrated with the spirit of Christ, who fills their whole lives..."(FC§56). These and other similar examples point to an understanding of grace which pervades all of life.

Second: the family is called the "domestic church"(FC§21), repeating and citing the term used for the family in the Second Vatican Council document *Lumen Gentium.* The family is also called the "church in miniature" (FC§49), a concept the document introduces by saying, "the Christian family constitutes a specific revelation and realization of ecclesial communion, and for this reason too, it can and should be called, 'the domestic church' " (FC§21). Implicit in the idea of family being called church is the concept of family being sacrament or sign of the presence of Jesus. As church is a sacrament, so the family, as domestic church, is a sacrament. And just as the church celebrates sacraments in the community, so does the family ritualize its gifts, its ups and downs, its brokenness, its giftedness. It celebrates its relationships. It experiences life everyday; at certain times such as birthdays, parties, Sunday dinners or brunches, it takes life in slow motion so its members can come to new realizations, new awarenesses of what they mean to each other. At such times families take their raw experiences, make them significant and celebrate them. This is the heart of sacramentality (Guzie, 1981). So I propose that by saying the family is "domestic church" the document is implying the family is sacrament.

Third: the notion of community which is integral to sacramental life is also critical to family life. The document states:

> Conjugal communion constitutes the foundation on which is built the broader communion of the family...This communion is rooted in the natural bonds of flesh and blood and grows to its specifically human perfection with the establishment and maturing of the still deeper and richer bonds of the spirit: The love that animates the interpersonal relationships of the different members of the family constitutes the interior strength that shapes and animates the family communion and community (FC§21).

A large amount of psychological research points to family as the first community or system where values are passed on. It is in the family where basic identity is usually assumed. It is the family who gives us saints by initiating and nourishing its members into Christian life. The community assembled for Eucharist is a major sign of the presence of the Lord. So also, the family community is a sign of the presence of the Lord.

While family is the most basic of communities, it is not a community unto itself. It needs to interact with and through other families and individuals and groups. The larger church community calls and challenges individual families to celebrate their identity and to grow through relationships with others beyond individual family membership. The document promotes families working with other families (FC§72). It sees the tasks of such relationships as fostering a sense of solidarity with other families, as favoring a life-style inspired by Gospel values, and as stimulating people to perform works of charity for one another.

At this point the importance of the family celebrating its sacramental dimension within the larger community needs to be recognized. In developing the notion of the sacramental dimension of family life, I am neither negating nor diminishing the importance of the celebration of sacraments in the larger church community. Both are needed. Sacramental life is a two-sided coin: one side focuses on the family relationships; the other, on the larger community. Each nurtures the other. One without the other is incomplete.

In fact, if the sacramental dimension of life is not recognized in the family, it is probably inadequately understood or misunderstood as celebrated in the seven sacraments of the Catholic Christian Church. If sacramentality is only seen in the family community, the family's potential for growth is inhibited and the possibility of stagnation increases. It may be impoverished because it will not be nourished by the richness of the traditions of the larger church community.

Fourth: the sacramental dimension of the family can be seen precisely in its reciprocal relationship to the larger church community. The document addresses two patterns of relationships between church and family. At one point it talks about the family enriching the larger church community:

> Inspired and sustained by the new commandment of love, the Christian family welcomes, respects and serves every human being, considering each one in his or her dignity as a person and as a child of God.
>
> It should be so especially between husband and wife and within the family through a daily effort to promote a truly personal community, initiated and fostered by an inner communion of love. This way of life should then be extended to the wider circle of the ecclesial community of which the Christian family is a part.
>
> Thanks to love within the family, the church can and ought to take on a more homelike or family dimension, developing a more human and fraternal style of relationships (FC§64).

At another point *Familiaris Consortio* speaks of the church proclaiming the good news to the family and challenging the family to develop its full potential for sacramentality:

> Christians also have the mission of proclaiming with joy and conviction the good news about the family, for the family absolutely needs to hear

ever anew and to understand ever more deeply the authentic words that reveal its identity, its inner resources and the importance of its mission in the city of God and in that of man (FC§86).

This dual relationsip is further alluded to:

> To the extent in which the Christian family accepts the Gospel and matures in faith, it becomes an evangelizing community...
> ...the future of evangelization depends in a great part on the church of the home (FC§52).

In summary, the family and the Church have an interdependent relationship as they participate in the Mission of Jesus.

Conclusion

Implicit in *Familiaris Consortio*, then, is the notion that the family is sacramental and celebrates its sacramentality within itself and within the larger community. In summary:

1. Grace is seen as permeating all life (FC§§21, 39, 56).
2. The family is recognized as the "domestic church" (FC§§21, 49, 52) thus implying participation in the sacramental dimension of Catholic Christianity.
3. Holiness is inherent in family life (FC§21). This is congruent with the church's theological understanding of sacramentality.
4. The family is seen to operate as community of system (FC§50). Community is an essential theological symbol of sacramentality.
5. Family and the larger church community are seen in a reciprocal relationship. This, in the context outlined above, implies that the larger church community is enriched by the sacramentality of the family and that the family is nurtured by the holiness present in the larger church community (FC§§64, 86, 50).

NOTES

1. Karl Rahner, S.J., "How to Receive A Sacrament and Mean It." *Theology Digest* Vol. 19, No. 3. Autumn, 97.

2. E. Schillebeeckx, OP, *Christ the Sacrament of the Encounter with God*. New York: Sheed and Ward. 1963.

3. Tad Guzie, *The Book of Sacramental Basics*. New York: Paulist Press, 1981.

2

Home Fires

Theological Reflections on the Christian Family

David M. Thomas, Ph. D.

REGIS COLLEGE, DENVER, COLORADO

"If I knew it was really worthwhile, I could endure almost anything." How many of us have said something like this when facing adversity, or just when trying to make it through an ordinary day? Knowing that one's efforts count or that someone appreciates your activity is enough. On the other hand, a sense that it's all meaningless, that one is just putting in time is sure to take the wind out of one's sails. I have begun this essay on the Christian family with a comment on meaning because I would like to help married Christians to better appreciate the worth and meaning inherent in their lives. I write also for myself as a husband and father with the intention of sharpening my own awareness of the meaning of my life as it unfolds from my domestic relationships.

Jesus came to expose meaning in all of life's circumstances. The "Kingdom within" is alive whenever life is valued and enriched; or, to paraphrase Paul: in eating and drinking and in whatever one does. From the standpoint of Christian faith, where the Lord is present, alive, and active, everything can be meaningful; nothing is ruled out. Faith in this context is not an affirmation of that which is distant, but the acceptance of that which is most near: God in the world, the Lord in everyday interpersonal relationships, the Spirit in every act of acknowledgment and kindness. A Christian interpretation is available for everything that happens to a family from morning til night, and even into the night.

But does the average mother and father, wife and husband, child and teen, have much sense of this? When the issue of personal spirituality is raised, do many people imagine scenes of the family around the dinner table, in front of the television set, or relaxing together in the living room? Recent papal teaching, particularly that of John Paul II's in *Familiaris Consortio*, has provided a resounding yes to the sacramental nature of family

15

experiences, although the impact of the teaching has been muted by the formal language in which it is stated. What follows, therefore, is my interpretation of five central texts in *Familiaris Consortio*. The five texts I have chosen to focus on are fundamental for the Christian life of the family. When integrated into a holistic framework, these five elements of family life provide both a structure for understanding and a direction for movement. Also I intend to structure this material into a framework directly applicable to the life of the family. For this purpose, I shall be guided by psychologist Erik Erikson, particularly by his descriptions of how to establish a sense of *identity*, experience the process of *intimacy*, and express the power of life-giving in *generativity*.

The Lord Jesus came to promise all the energy and power needed to live out life's multiple demands, as well as to reveal to humanity the nature of the Divine Mystery, in which life here on earth is unfolded. He underscored the worthwhile nature of life, called for endurance, and promised life in even more abundance. To individuals and families, some of this deserves retelling; and the church as teacher continues to accept this as a basic mandate. Some people today doubt the viability of the Christian family as a community of love and fidelity. It is, therefore, all the more urgent that the church express a message of hope for the survival of the family, the most basic community of the church.

IDENTIFICATION OF THE FAMILY AS CHURCH

I find no other idea in the church's teaching on the family more supportive and challenging than the outright acknowledgment that the Christian family itself is a central embodiment of the church. This has come to be described under various titles in formal church teaching. Sometimes the family is referred to as "the domestic church," "the church of the home," "the household of faith," or "the church in miniature (*ecclesiola*)." These titles all point to the same fact: the family itself is part of the church. It has the same functions as the rest of the church, but it is the church in a family way (FC§49).

Naming the family itself as an ecclesial community brings the family, so to speak, within the ambit of the church and avoids by implication all thinking that draws an absolute distinction between the family and the church. All events of the family are, therefore, church events. They are all drawn into the dynamics of building the Kingdom.

This also means that the family cannot be thought of as having only an earthly meaning. This falsely separates the family from other expressions of church life. The family stands under the power and the judgment of grace and, for many, the more significant events of their religious life occur *within* the family,

Pastoral strategy need not place the concerns of the family over against those of the parish or diocese. The life of the church is, before all else, a communal happening. And the family ordinarily plays a more important role in the communal life of people, which suggests that pastoral priority should be given to its needs. We are brought to salvation through the hearing of the Word of God, and much of the capacity to understand and accept that Word will come from the experiential development established through family relationships.

Evangelization, catechesis, worship, and ministry will all have their family expressions; but because of the earthly character of family life, they will be rather secular in appearance. Evangelization will involve the communication of trust expressed through affirming embraces and gestures of forgiveness. These arise amidst the mundane tasks of getting meals on the table, cleaning rooms, and playing ball in the backyard. Worship will be expressed in meal prayers, in expressions of gratitude for safe returns, or, as the writing of John Paul II explicitly notes, in the celebration of birthdays in the family. Ministry will encompass the countless acts of "helping out," whether this means washing dishes or dirty faces, or any action of cooperation or caring that brings people closer together in the family.

Identifying the family as church inaugurates a new way of thinking and perceiving for many people. It jars the religious images which limit divine realities to formal religion and to those events which only take place in church buildings. In the church of the home, all family members are priests by virtue of baptism, and all celebrate the liturgy of the home through the daily fabric of family exchange. For it is the *life* of the family itself which is its basic spiritual resource. And it is the way in which the love of God and neighbor are joined together in the family that give it its most fundamental charge.

INTIMACY IN LOVE AS THE LIFE OF THE FAMILY

Once the family is given its proper name, the next task is to describe its basic task or mission. John Paul II describes this mission of the family: "…to guard, reveal, and communicate love, and this is a living reflection of and a real sharing in God's love for humanity and the love of Christ the Lord for the church, his bride" (FC§17). Another way of describing this is to speak about the task of witnessing the reality of divine love become human in family relationships.

To describe all the features of family love would take a book. It should at least be noted that family love is quite down-to-earth, based on knowing the one who is loved, and loving the one who is known. This love is tied to those exchanges and actions that form much of the basis of human survival. It is largely based on daily decisions to accept and affirm those closest to us. It is faithful and forgiving, and, to put it briefly, it is quite demanding.

Family love is a special instance of God's love breaking into human relationships. God's love is persistent, constant, and affirming. It is these qualities of love that have a particular bearing on family relationships. In a sense, love in the family, the love between spouses and between children and parents is an acid test for genuineness. Family love calls forth a kind of loving that requires commitment and action. This is not mentioned to degrade the emotional or even sentimental aspects of love. The more that love is allowed to fill one's life, the harder it will be to locate love in only one part of the person or in one area of life. The joining of love with life is a special feature of the intimacy proper within the family, and it is this feature that deserves special consideration.

LOVE GIVING BIRTH TO LIFE

Familiaris Consortio states that, "...love and life constitute the nucleus of the saving mission of the Christian family in the church and for the church"(FC§50). This formulation reminds us of the teaching of Vatican II that the procreative meaning of marriage is based on the generative power of marital love. The theme that love generates and nourishes life is not only a sound principle for human development but it also mirrors the underlying process of divine, creative generativity. From God's love, creation came to be. From God's faithful love creation continues. It is the same within the Christian family. If the focus is on the procreative side of marriage, new life is explained not so much as rooted in an instinct for continuing the species, but as an expression of love between wife and husband and, once children have been brought into the family, as an expression of family generativity. The decision to bring futher life into the family should be based on a consideration of existing family members.

Bringing life to individuals and doing all that is necessary to nourish and enrich that life is part of this expression of love in a life-affirming way. We have already mentioned that family life touches the basics of human survival. Family life lays down foundations for both bodily and spiritual growth. When the family is described as a "community of persons," this implies a holistic appreciation of the person, wherein spirit and body are joined. Providing healthy food on the family table makes possible the eventual reception of the food called Eucharist. Receiving the Eucharist can bring about an appreciation of the deeper meaning of food in other settings, particularly when food is eaten in loving community around the family table. This does not imply that family meals mimic Eucharistic meals in the parish church. Although I can imagine an improvement in some parish liturgies if they took on more of a family spirit.

The point here is that a Christian appreciation of the family will be built on an appreciation of the processes through which life comes to be and is nourished toward growth in God's sight. Furthermore, love is necessary for life to become all that it might be. This may be a principle that is central to secular wisdom, but it is also directly applicable to the Christian life. The blending of the love of life and the life of love is nowhere more significant than within the family where life is so vulnerable and needs the protection of trusting and open love.

EVANGELIZATION: FAMILY STYLE

The basic word of evangelization is this: You are loved! But it is not enough simply to say this word. The word demands flesh; it requires actions of love to demonstrate in human ways that the person is indeed loved. Each person ordinarily (although not always) first experiences being loved in the family. Thus John Paul II is moved to write about the role of the family in the process of evangelization: "The Christian family, in fact, is the first community called to announce the Gospel to the human person during growth and to bring him or her, through a progressive education and catechesis, to full human and Christian maturity" (FC§2). Further on in the same document he adds that the parental role in evangelization is "original and irreplaceable" (FC§53).

I must add a word of caution to prevent a reduction of the evangelical process to simply the dynamics which operate between parent and child. What is being described is the unfolding process wherein the love described above is present and effective in the lives of both parent and child. However, we all know of situations where love is absent and where the child does not experience being loved in the home. This can only be described as a tragedy. Yet exceptions ought not vitiate the rule, and these failures need not rule out the possibility of success in other relationships.

The process is not one-sided because the child has the reciprocal capacity to send the same message to the parent. Paul VI expressed this idea in his writing on evangelization when he noted that, "In a family which is conscious of this mission, all the members evangelize and are evangelized." (*Evangelii Nuntiandi*—On Evangelization in the Modern World, §71) Students of family dynamics who take what is called a systems approach to family life know something about this principle. For them the family is an organic "body" with mutual causality and exchanges taking place among all the family members. The messages that are sent within the family, both verbal and non-verbal, are more than those of mom or dad, daughter or son. They carry the message that Christ Jesus came to earth to proclaim. The family community of the church is the first to have the opportunity to speak the Gospel, to express, in touch and tone, the good news, "You are loved." Eventually the mature person will sort out the various sources of love, and hopefully will come to the realization that family love, while first to announce the Gospel to the child, was not first, in fact, because it was God's love which brought the family itself into being and stands with it as its ongoing source for endurance.

THE FAMILY'S GIFT TO THE WIDER COMMUNITY

Before Pope John Paul's letter on the family was issued, it would have been difficult to think of the family in any other role than that of receiver of the spiritual riches of the wider church. The sacramental life of the church was available primarily in the parish church; the educational services came from the parish school or religious education program; the ministers of the church were mostly priests and religious. The family received its spiritual nourishment from outside its own boundaries. Families went to church.

We saw a break in that formulation when the Christian family was recognized as a true and significant embodiment of the church itself. To find the church, the family could look to itself, and while more of the church may be on the outside, some of it was on the inside. I have suggested that this is a significant change for the religious or ecclesial imagination, and it will no doubt take much time and serious reflection to mine the full riches of this insight. It should also be added that some people may not be happy to hear that many of the major demands of their religious life now rest within the confines of their own family.

But even more is said by the pope in his invitation to the wider church to receive from the family what it can offer. The direction has been reversed. The wider church is now going to the family to become more fully what it is supposed to be, a community of love. John Paul II writes, "Thanks to love within the family, the church can and ought to take on a more homelike or family dimension, developing a more human and fraternal style of relationships" (FC§64).

This provides the family with the challenge of letting itself be known to the outside. It is also saying that the life of family is constitutive of the life of the whole church. The love existing in the family, for better or worse, ends up being its interior principle of vitality. In the beginning of his exhortation on the family, John Paul II notes that strong families make strong societies. Toward the conclusion of his letter, he affirms much the same about the life of the church. The fire of the Spirit of love exists within the family, and both church and society need this for warmth and energy. He might have concluded his discussion of the Christian family with a call to keep the home fires burning. He didn't, but I will, because it is in the setting of the family that many of my co-Christians now experience the energy of God more intently than in any other setting of church life. The experience does not prompt one to guard that treasure from the outsider, but rather to open the doors of the family to welcome the stranger into this special setting of God's love.

3

Familiaris Consortio

A Review of Its Theology

Michael D. Place, STD

THE ATHENAEUM OF OHIO
CINCINNATI, OHIO

One of the givens of contemporary Roman Catholic theology is that just as scripture cannot be read uncritically or literally, so too magisterial statements are in need of contextualization and interpretation.[1] The reason is clear. Magisterial statements do not exist in a vacuum but are situated within a history of thought and action and often are part of an ongoing dialogue. This is especially true of magisterial statements related to the Synod of Bishops.[2] The topic of the synod is chosen because it reflects an ecclesial need. The synod is prepared for through a variety of consultative processes that occur nationally and internationally. The synod itself elicits a multitude of interventions, and issues a concluding report or document. And in the case of the 1980 synod, the synodal process was brought to a close with the papal exhortation *Familiaris Consortio*.

But what would be the best way to critically examine the theology of this document? One could compare it to other magisterial statements, or to the synodal interventions, or to the concluding propositions of the synod, or to the allocutions of John Paul II.[3] All of this could and should be done. However, in reflecting on the setting of this symposium—an American Catholic center of higher learning and education—it struck me that a more appropriate way to analyze the theology of *Familiaris Consortio* would be to set it in the context of another part of the dialogue of which it is a part; namely, the work of contemporary Catholic theologians. And in such a context, it is fair to say that Catholic theologians and canonists from the United States have made a significant contribution to the contemporary ecclesial discussion about marriage and family.[4] Because of the breadth of issues addressed both in the exhortation and in the work of the theologians, it will be necessary to limit this analysis.[5]

It is evident that there are three issues which in themselves do not directly pertain to the theology of marriage but which involve presuppositions that will affect significantly the development of a theology of marriage. They are theological methodology, an ecclesiological perspective, and an understanding of moral values or norms. After a review of the manner in which the exhortation discusses these issues, four theological topics relating to marriage will be reviewed: the meaning of Christian marriage, the significance of human sexuality, the sacramentality of Christian marriage, and the church's response to marital failure. The format of each consideration will be a summary of the manner in which certain theologians have been addressing the issue, a presentation of the papal position, and a comparison of the two. The conclusion will contain some observations about where the dialogue can go from here.

THEOLOGICAL METHODOLOGY

Perhaps one of the most important but subtle debates within Roman Catholic theology has centered on the manner in which the theological enterprise is approached. Recent writing has reflected on the impact of the scholastic method and in particular that of the nineteenth century neo-scholastic revival on the formulation of theological positions.[6] Both Bernard Lonergan and David Tracy have raised the question whether there is not a need to shift from what is described as a "classicist" perspective to an "historicist" perspective.[7]

The classicist perspective involves a methodology that is primarily deductive in nature. It begins with certain eternal and immutable truths that are accepted as the basis for any statements that might follow. In such an approach, there is little room for history or change to be of significance. The historicist perspective is more inductive in nature. Though it does not deny the ability to arrive at meaning or truth, it does make greater provision for the significance of the concrete, historical moment and does not see change as peripheral to the discovery of meaning or truth.

On first reading, it would appear that the exhortation has embraced this shift. The pope affirms that, "...the call and demands of the spirit resound in the very moments of history, and so the church can also be guided to a more profound understanding of the inexhaustible mystery of marriage and the family by the circumstances, the questions, and the anxieties and hopes of the young people, married couples, and parents of today" (FC§4). This recognition of the movement of the spirit in time is coupled with an image of the human person as one who advances "gradually with the progressive integration of the gifts of God and the demands of His definitive and absolute love..." (FC§9).

A more careful reading would suggest that while this recognition of the historical and this acknowledgment of the exigencies of change is real, it stands side by side in the papal reflections with the older methodology. At critical moments in the line of argumentation, there is a return to a description of a "divine plan," which gives a specificity to the inductive reasoning far beyond its own inner logic. A specific example can be found in the discussion on the meaning of sexuality. Sexuality is seen as an expression of a total self-giving, but that self-giving is immediately qualified by the phrase "through acts which are proper and exclusive to spouses" (FC§11). I do not say that this might not be the case, but rather suggest that this is asserted without any justification.

Thus it is that the text shows a sensitivity to a new perspective, but the adherents to that perspective might suggest that it does so in a manner that often returns to an older methodology in order to arrive at its conclusions.

ECCLESIOLOGICAL PERSPECTIVE

Intimately related to the question of theological methodology is the perspective from which one understands the meaning of church and the role of its various members in the discernment of the meaning of Christian living. Historical studies have revealed that the present self-understanding of the church and the relationships between the various offices and ministries is a "time-bound" understanding. There have been suggestions that the present dominant image of ecclesial life is too readily defined by a juridical or legalistic perspective which fails to recognize the diverse gifts of the ecclesial fellowship.[8] Of particular concern is the proper relationship of the theologian to the magisterial teaching of pope and bishops. The writings of theologians on these issues today make it clear that many of them ascribe a greater competency to the life and experience of the individual Catholic in matters of faith and morals than formerly was the practice.[9] Likewise, the role of the theologian is recognized as having a unique magisterial competency of its own—without denying the authoritative nature of the episcopal-papal magisterium.[10]

This shift in perspective is very much evident in the first part of the exhortation. Consistent with an approach that is more inductive in nature, the pope does not speak of a process of imposition of truth but rather of an "evangelical discernment" that offers an orientation toward the world which will preserve and realize the dignity of marriage (FC§§4,5). This discernment is done through a sense of faith "which is a gift that the Spirit gives to all the faithful." Because of this giftedness, "the church...does not accomplish this discernment only through the pastors...but also through the laity." And the laity engage in this discernment in order to interpret the history of the world in the light of Christ (FC§5).

In this initial recognition of the various movements of the Spirit, the pope does not lose sight of the authoritative role of the church's pastors. He is quick to point out that this sense of faith does not consist "solely or necessarily" in the consensus of the faithful. Sociological and statistical research is "not to be considered in itself an expression of the sense of faith" (FC§5). It is for that reason that there is an apostolic ministry that promotes the sense of faith, examines and authoritatively judges the genuiness of its expression, and educates the faithful in evangelical discernment.

This discussion of ecclesiological questions in general is sensitive to the theological posture outlined above. As the document develops, however, there seems to be a return to an ecclesiological language, if not perspective, that is more akin to a pre-Vatican II mentality or at least to a form of articulation that is problematic for many. Particularly striking is the description in the section on "Agents of Pastoral Care" of the relationship between pastors and the laity in the exercise of the prophetic mission of Christ. The laity are viewed as witnessing to the faith by their words and Christian lives. The pastors exercise their mission "by distinguishing in that witness what is the expression of genuine faith from what is less in harmony with the light of faith..." (FC§73). In this expression the nuanced complexity of the earlier articulation is lost, and the previous theological posture of the pastors teaching and the people listening seems to return.

This reaffirmation of an older ecclesiological perspective, which seems to minimize any possibility of legitimate tension or dialogue arising from a pluralism of charisms, is also found in the document's description of the role of the theologian. Rather than acknowledging the honest divergence of opinion on various questions which are addressed in the exhortation, the pope re-echos Pius XII's description of the proper function of the theologian when he asks theologians to commit themselves "to the task of illustrating ever more clearly the biblical foundations, the ethical grounds, and the personalistic reasons behind this doctrine" (FC§31).[11]

Thus it would seem that while the pope is anxious to affirm a more nuanced and developed ecclesiology emerging from the work of Vatican II, he also is still able to repeat an earlier ecclesiology. How the two postures are to be reconciled is difficult for many theologians to see.

MORAL VALUES OR NORMS

Integrally related to the questions of theological methodology and ecclesiological perspective is the problem of how to articulate and understand
moral guidelines and the correlative question of the relationship of the
individual to such guidelines.

Recently, a significant part of the theological community has experienced a qualitative development in its undertanding of the role and function of moral guidelines and the place of individual responsibility.[12] While
not denying that there is an objective order of morality to which all human
beings and believing Christians are called to conform, today the articulation of that moral order is understood as being more complicated than before. For these theologians, the reality of human finitude and sinfulness
are not seen as having destroyed the human condition but as having made
conflict between 'goods,' or values, inevitable. As a result, it is not possible
for the human person to achieve all goods in all situations, and at times
various goods can be in conflict.[13]

The acceptance of this conflictual state of the human condition by some
theologians has resulted in a disagreement between those theologians who
see the human vocation as being "the maximizing of the good and the min-
imizing of the bad" and those who hold to an older perspective which as-
serts that in some situations there is a particular good that must be realized
no matter what the conflict. Or to put it in more technical language, there
are those who recognize the complexity of the human situation and assert
that one must evaluate the appropriateness of moral activity by analyzing
all of the components of the situation: the act, the circumstances, and the
end. Those who hold this opinion believe that no single component can
determine the rightness or wrongness of a human action. The other position proposes that while this might be acceptable in some moral situations,
there are others where the rightness or wrongness of an activity is determined by the nature of the act itself. Thus it is that some acts are considered
to be "intrinsically evil."

While this disagreement is on the level of how moral values are described, it also has bearing on the living of the Christian life. While ad-
hering to the traditional Catholic belief that one is called to grow in the
meaning of a Christian life that has a specific content to it, many moral
theologians recognize the unique role of the individual conscience and the
fact that growth in the moral life is a life-long process.[14] Of its nature, the
present human condition precludes the possibility of a full realization of
the ideals which were preached and lived by Christ. The recognition that
the human family is living in the eschatological tension of searching for an

ideal that is not yet, provides room for a pastoral response in certain situations that would differ from that of theologians of another perspective. Whether justified by the theory of compromise or through other categories, an individual could be seen as being in "good faith" and not living in complete conformity with certain Christian ideals. [15]

It is obvious that some of the insights of this moral perspective have been recognized in the writing of the papal text. The conflictual nature of human existence is described as an interplay of light and darkness. History is not a fixed progression "toward what is better, but rather an event of freedom, and even a struggle between freedoms that are in mutual conflict..."(FC§6). In this vein, the condition of the human person is seen as historical and in process; thus it can be said that the human person "is an historical being who day by day builds himself up through his many free decisions; and so he knows, loves, and accomplishes moral good by stages of growth"(FC§34).

This recognition of conflict and growth by the Holy Father is limited, however. He clearly separates himself from the newer perspective on the conflictual nature of moral values when he reasserts the teaching of Vatican II on birth control, which says that "...the moral aspect of any procedure does not depend solely on sincere intentions or an evaluation of motives. It must be determined by objective standards" (FC§32). By objective standards, he means the nature of the act of intercourse. The same approach will be seen later in his discussion of marital failure.

This disagreement also is evident in his consideration of the implications of moral growth. Moral law is not "an ideal to be achieved in the future." Rather, it is "a...command of Christ to ovecome difficulties with constancy." He goes on to say "what is known as the 'law of gradualness' or step-by-step advance cannot be identified with 'gradualness of law', as if there were different degrees or forms of precept in God's law for different individuals and situations" (FC§34). While recognizing the reality of conflict and the difficulty of achieving the ideal, he suggests that it is not possible to achieve the resurrection without the cross and that sacrifice cannot be removed from life. It is the task of church to call people to such sacrifice and nourish and strengthen them in their struggle.

It is this disagreement about the meaning of moral values and their relationship to the life journey of each Christian that will serve as a foundation for other variances between the position of some Catholic theologians and the teaching of this papal exhortation. It would be unfair to focus on the particularity of some of the other discussions because the real debate is in this area of moral norms and absolutes.

THE MEANING OF CHRISTIAN MARRIAGE

Previous to the time of Vatican II, the Catholic perspective on marriage was very much defined by a legal or canonical interpretation. Much of the foundational theology on the sacrament of marriage was developed during a time in the life of the church that was dominated by its "jurist" popes.[16] Moreover, the manuals, which communicated moral and sacramental teaching in the fifty years before Vatican II, were written under the guidance of church law. The result was that the church spoke of and understood marriage in terms of a contract. For the contract to be valid, there had to be: competent parties, apt matter, the proper intention, the ability to fulfill the terms of the contract, and an appropriate signing of the contract.[17]

In recent years there has been a movement away from this view. Influenced by the personalist and existential thought of Western Europe, Catholic theologians came to speak of marriage as a covenant rather than a contract. The purpose or meaning of that covenant was seen as the establishment of a community of life and love between the couple; and this was expressed and celebrated in an openness to life. Gone was the extensive debate over primary or secondary ends of marriage and the impression that the only purpose for marriage was the bearing of children.[18]

Similar to the move to a non-juridical understanding of marriage itself was the questioning of the historical belief that marriage had about it a unitative dimension which was to last for life. Many began to suggest that while the value of such permanence was an essential ingredient of Christian marriage, the concept of indissolubility, which expressed that permanence, was as inadequate to the mystery of marital permanence as the concept of contract was to the mystery of marital union. The suggestion was made that a movement away from the physical imagery of the *vinculum*, or bond of indissolubility, toward the idea of a moral ideal or ethical imperative would be more faithful to the Christian belief.[19]

In some of these areas the papal exhortation clearly reflects the movement which has taken place in theological circles. The primary source of reflection on the meaning of Christian marriage is not a legal category but the very mystery of the Godhead. The reasoning is easy to follow. Humans are made in the image of God and thus share in the meaning of a divine plan (FC§§11,17). It is the meaning of the divine that gives shape and direction to what is human. And that meaning is: "God is love, and in Himself He lives a mystery of personal loving communion"(FC§11). The human person is given the capacity and responsibility of such love and communion.

Setting aside for the moment the detailed analysis of the question of sexuality, it is necessary to point out that, according to the text, this vocation to the love and communion of the Godhead can be expressed either in marriage or celibacy. In marriage, the total physical self-giving of conjugal love is akin to the intimate community of life and love that is willed by God. The only place in which love is possible is in marriage. Marriage is the interior requirement for the covenant of conjugal love that is publicly affirmed as unique and faithful.

While this covenanted love, which requires marriage as its necessary conclusion, reflects the inner life of the Godhead, there is another dimension to the Godhead: its relationship with the human family. In this relationship, God is seen as being ever faithful. This fidelity is especially revealed in the covenant of God with the people of Israel and becomes the "model of the relations of faithful love that should exist between spouses"(FC§12). Because marriage is a reflection of the inner and outer life of the Godhead, it naturally is a covenanted and faithful love that unites two persons together for life.

This inner meaning is brought to fulfillment in Christ and his sacrificial union with humankind and the church. In Christ, man and woman are given the capacity to live as he did, and the plan "which God has imprinted on the humanity of man and woman since creation" is revealed (FC§13). Conjugal love reaches a fullness to which it is ordered, conjugal charity; and because it is a participation in the spousal love of Christ, it is sacramental in nature. For that reason, marriage between two Christians has been considered one of the seven sacraments of church life and understood to be indissoluble.

In this discussion of the basic meaning of Christian marriage, the pope again has caught the flavor of the contemporary theological discussion. By moving into the interiority of the life of the Godhead, in fact, he has given greater depth to the communitarian dimension of marital love. The clear association of marriage with the movement of divine faithfulness gives a firm foundation to the permanency and sacramentality of Christian marriage.

In the same way, the document goes a long way to rectify an exaggerated view of the relationship of childbearing to marital life. On the one hand, the pope proposes that the fruitfulness, which is to be part of marital life, is not be to be restricted solely to the procreation of children, but "is enlarged and enriched by all those fruits of moral, spiritual, and supernatural life which the father and mother are called to hand on to their children, and through the children to the church and to the world"(FC§28). On the other hand, in speaking of physical sterility, he says that "even when procreation is not possible, conjugal life does not for this reason lose its value" (FC§14). In fact, it can be the occasion for other important services to the life of the human person.

Though these correctives are present, the more traditional emphasis on the procreative aspect of marriage is not lost. Early in the document, he proclaims that "the very institution of marriage and conjugal love is ordained to the procreation and education of children, in whom it finds its crowning" (FC§14). Though this unnuanced assertion is later contextualized by the Vatican II concern not to make "the other purposes of matrimony of less account," he affirms with Vatican II that "the true practice of conjugal love and the whole meaning of family life which results from it, have this aim: that the couple be ready with stout hearts to cooperate with the love of the creator and savior, who through them will enlarge and enrich His own family day by day" (FC§28).

Reviewing the papal theology, one sympathetic to the recent theological concerns would raise certain questions. For example, because of the clear and repeated affirmation in the past of the unique ordering of marriage towards childbearing, has there been any attempt to reconcile the tension between a communion of life and love, which is the pope's basic image of marriage, with the demands of childbearing. After reading the full text, one wonders whether the prior category of the primary end of marriage as procreation has really been replaced by the primacy of a community of life and love.

Similarly, though the argumentation for the unity and permanence of marriage originates in the faithfulness of God toward all people, is it clear that the concept of indissolubility is the most apt expression of that unity and permanence? Or is the use of indissolubility in part influenced by the primacy of childbearing? The reason for the question is that if we accept the primary meaning for permanence as being rooted in divine fidelity, then the justification for indissolubility contains a second reason: the good of children (FC§20). Without denying that children need a stable familial setting, is that need of the same significance as the fidelity of Christ to his church? Is it possible that there could be other needs on the part of the children that are equal to or at times greater than such stability? If so, how do they relate to the concept of indissolubility? Finally, in the context of marriage that is understood in personal and communal terms, how can one use the impersonal and juridical category of indissolubility to describe interpersonal fidelity? These and other questions reflect a significant distance between this part of the papal exhortation and the work of contemporary theology.

THE SIGNIFICANCE OF HUMAN SEXUALITY

It is no secret that for many centuries the Catholic tradition in regard to human sexuality was marked by dualism and negativity. Within much of Catholic writing there was a suspicion of a dichotomy between the corporeal and spiritual dimensions of a person. It was the spiritual dimension which was more divine-like, therefore it was implied that corporeality was less than good. Because sexuality is experienced as something very much related to the body, it was often viewed as a necessary evil of the human condition and was justified only in the context of the procreation of off-spring. The specific ethic which developed this perspective was equally negative in orientation and actuality. The only appropriate context of sex-uality and sexual activity was that of marriage. In line with this approach, celibacy was viewed as a better or higher vocation than marriage.[20]

Consistent with the other developments in Catholic theology, there has been a move away from this dualism and negativity. The human person is now viewed as a totality whose life project is to integrate all parts of one's being. Human sexuality is no longer identified with the genital function but is essentially related to the distinctively human capacity for, and drive toward, intimacy. In such a context, sexuality is a basic human good and is devoid of all taint of evil. (Though like all human goods, it is capable of misuse.)[21]

When viewed in this manner and placed in the context of the newer understanding of moral values or norms, sexuality and sexual activity are evaluated in a very different fashion. Though there is no consensus on the terms of the analysis, many moral theologians have come to ethical conclu-sions on issues such as masturbation, pre-marital sexuality, birth control, and homosexuality that are at variance with earlier stances. Likewise, the meaning of celibacy or virginity is expressed differently.

Once again, the papal document reflects an awareness of this newer understanding of human sexuality. In unequivocal terms it moves away from the exaggerated dualism of the past when it describes the human vocation to love as the vocation of a "unified totality" (FC§11). "Love in-cludes the human body, and the body is made a sharer in spiritual love." Sexuality is not something tainted by its embodiment, but "concerns the innermost being of the human person as such"(FC§11). While not speaking directly of intimacy, the pope describes sexuality as only being truly human if it is "an integral part of the love by which a man and woman unite them-selves totally to one another until death"(FC§11).

Where the document diverges from contemporary writing is in its apparent identification of sexuality with marriage, and in particular with fertility. Though all people are called to a vocation of love, the pope only mentions "two ways of realizing" this vocation: "marriage and virginity or celibacy"(FC§11). But sexuality is only realized "in a truly human way" in the marital union. The obvious question of the newer theological stance described above is What does this say about the sexuality of those who are not in a marital union? Is their sexuality to be expressed or experienced in a less than human way? If the only 'place' in which this self-giving "in its whole truth is made possible is marriage," then is the love of a celibate or non-married person less than the whole truth? (FC§11)

When the logic of this first discussion is placed alongside the explicit discussion of celibacy or virginity, the papal answers to the above question become more apparent. In comparing marriage and celibacy, the pope says that "when human sexuality is not regarded as a great value given by the creator, the *renunciation of it* for the sake of the kingdom of heaven loses its meaning"(FC§16). Though the Holy Father goes on to suggest that the meaning of celibacy is to give witness to and support of marriage, because celibacy gives witness to the "eschatological marriage of Christ with the church...."; it would seem that the celibate or consecrated virgin is one who has left sexuality behind. In suggesting this renunciation, the document has returned to an understanding of sexuality that is rather physical in nature and specifically identified with the genital. This assumption is complicated, however, by the later assertion that celibacy is "the supreme form of that self-giving that constitutes the very meaning of sexuality"(FC§37). At the very least, the relationship between sexuality and intimacy with the celibate life is not self-evident.

Besides being concerned about this rather "asexual"notion of celibacy, some theologians wonder whether this line of reasoning provides any explanation of the place of sexuality in the life of the unmarried who are not called to celibacy or consecrated virginity. Especially in the United States and other Western nations, the numbers of such people are growing. And the document provides no theoretical foundation for the meaning of their lives.

At the same time, the document continues the historical affirmation that, because of its eschatological witness, the charism of celibacy is superior to that of marriage "by reason of the wholly singular link which it has with the kingdom of God" (FC§16). Many theologians would be uncomfortable with the identification of one charism as superior to another, especially when the very nature of marriage has been identified in this document as reflective of the inner life of the Godhead. Is it not possible to say that both charisms are divine calls, without the prioritization which seems to resurrrect the old dualism?

Turning to the specific ethical imperatives that flow from this theoretical posture, the exhortation unequivocally affirms the teaching of *Humanae Vitae*. This begins with an affirmation of the values which are to be present within marital love and marital sexuality. The love "between husband and wife must be fully human, exclusive, and open to new life"(FC§29).

The proper expression of these values requires that there can be no breaking of the "inseparable connection willed by God... between the two meanings of the conjugal act: the unitive meaning and the procreative meaning" (FC§32). For that reason, he reasserts that an act is intrinsically immoral that "either in anticipation of the conjugal act, or in its accomplishment, or in the development of its natural consequences, proposes, whether as an end or as a means, to render procreation impossible" (FC§32).

This affirmation of the intrinsic evil of birth control and sterilization not only affirms the papal adherence to a vision of moral norms and values that were mentioned above, but it also gives implicit support to the specific ethical conclusions which have been applied to the question of masturbation, pre-marital sexuality, and homosexuality. Such conclusions have been, and will remain, a source of tension between papal teaching and the writings of many moral theologians.

THE SACRAMENTALITY OF CHRISTIAN MARRIAGE

As we noted above, the present theology and discipline of marriage is very much a product of an age when the ecclesial experience and cultural experience were one—the age of Christendom. In that world, all who were baptized were assumed to be believers, and all who believed were capable of, and intended to do, what the church intended. Within this perspective, the church's belief—that all those who were baptized and celebrated a marriage had necessarily contracted a valid sacramental union—made perfect sense.[22]

In recent years, however, many theologians have questioned this assumption. It should be clear that the theologians have not questioned whether a true Christian marriage is sacramental, but only *when* a marriage is sacramental. (The manner in which the permanency is associated with that sacramentality is questioned, however.) The reason for the recent concern is that in many parts of the Western world baptism has become more of a social event than a celebration of faith. And so baptized Catholics may approach marriage without what many theologians would consider to be a true faith in the Christian mysteries. Without such faith, theologians ask whether there can be a sacramental and permanent union. Implicit in this discussion is a re-examination of the meaning of Christian faith. Consistent with the movement to think of the human person in a wholistic and developmental fashion, there has been a move to understand faith not in mechanistic terms but as a lived reality in which a person is called to move from an immature to mature possession.[23]

The pastoral conclusions of this thinking have been significant. First, there is the acknowledgement that there can be a baptized person who, in fact, is not a believer and therefore is incapable of a sacramental union. Second, there can be baptized Catholics who wish to get married but who are not at a level of faith possession that would allow them to live a Christian sacramental union in its full meaning. Third, marriage should be prepared for with a care and pastoral strategy that will help the couple move from a less mature to a more mature understanding of its meaning and toward the ability to celebrate marriage in its Christian fullness. Where such movement does not occur, then marriage should be delayed.[24]

The Holy Father, in his reflections on the pastoral care of the family, recognizes the change in emphasis which these discussions have precipitated. Noting that we live in a secularized society, he acknowledges that the "faith of the person asking the church for marriage can exist in different degrees..." (FC§68). For that reason, he strongly urges that there should be a time of preparation for marriage, which is a type of "journey of faith which is similar to the catechumenate" (FC§66). Such a journey is a gradual and continuous process with three main stages: remote, proximate, and immediate. Though this preparation is primarily meant to prepare the couple for entering the marriage union, it is also to assist the couple in seeing that their union is an interpersonal relationship that is "to be continually developed."

Though recognizing the developmental nature of faith and the various levels of peoples' readiness for marriage, the pope draws some conclusions that would challenge certain pastoral strategies. While he calls for a period of preparation, saying that one "must not underestimate the necessity and obligation of immediate preparation for marriage," he goes on to say that such preparation should be put in practice "in such a way that omitting it is not an impediment to the celebration of marriage" (FC§66).

Similarly, though he recognizes the different levels of faith possession, the pope tells pastors that they must also understand "the reasons that lead the church to admit to the celebration of marriage those who are imperfectly disposed" (FC§68). The reasoning behind this conclusion is interesting. In line with his earlier description of marriage, he suggests that marriage is part of the very economy of creation and the decision of a couple to marry "in accordance with this divine plan... really involves, even if not in a fully conscious way, an attitude of profound obedience to the will of God, an attitude which cannot exist without God's grace." This possibility of right intention enlightened by grace means that those who are baptized "at least implicitly, consent to what the church intends to do when she celebrates marriage" (FC§68). The conclusion of this reasoning would be that ordinarily it is impossible to have a union of two baptized persons that is not sacramental in nature. This is affirmed in a later section when the pope speaks against trial marriages, saying that "between two baptized persons there can exist only an indissoluble marriage"(FC§80).

Implicit in this stance is a rejection of the pastoral practice, which has developed in some areas, of distinguishing between different types of unions which Christians might celebrate. In this practice, only those who are fully prepared to celebrate the integral meaning of marriage would be allowed to enter a sacramental union. For those not so prepared, a different non-sacramental ceremony would be celebrated. Though his focus is on the reality of Catholics who celebrate a merely civil marriage, the pope opposes this practice when he speaks against baptized Catholics entering into any union that is not fully sacramental. Though he recognizes that such unions reflect the desire of a couple to accept not only the advantages but also the obligations of marriage, he says that "nevertheless, not even this situation is acceptable to the church"(FC§82). It should be noted, however, that while he affirms the impropriety of a Catholic entering into a non-sacramental union and discourages any other unions for the baptized, he does say that whenever a couple "reject explicitly and formally what the church intends to do when the marriage of baptized persons is celebrated, the pastor of souls cannot admit them to the celebration of marriage"(FC§68).

As in other sections of the exhortation, it is difficult for many theologians to reconcile the pope's recognition of certain theological and pastoral developments with his refusal to accept consequent changes in pastoral practice. Many of those who are actively involved in parochial ministry would question the necessity of maintaining the identification of sacramentality with the union of two baptized Christians regardless of their level of faith. Likewise, the resorting to an "implicit" or unconscious faith is viewed as not being consistent with the principles of faith development and maturation that is called for in the new Rite of Christian Initiation of Adults. They would argue that it would be better to respond with a pastoral practice that would recognize the diversity of those approaching marriage, rather than insisting on a sacramental marriage or no marriage at all. In this instance, the pope is rather clear in why he wishes to affirm his view:

> As for wishing to lay down further criteria for admission to the ecclesial celebration of marriage, criteria that would concern the level of faith of those to be married, this would above all involve grave risks. In the first place, the risk of making unfounded and discriminatory judgments; second, the risk of causing doubts about the validity of marriages already celebated, with grave harm to Christian communities and new and unjustified anxieties to the consciences of married cou-

ples; one would also fall into the danger of calling into question the sacramental nature of many marriages of brethren separated from full communion with the Catholic Church, thus contradicting ecclesial tradition (FC§68).

Whether the citing of these risks will convince those who have raised the concerns noted above is not evident.

RESPONSE TO MARITAL FAILURE

Many of the developments outlined above come to a very concrete articulation in the way in which the church responds to those who experience marital failure. The understanding of the meaning of church and the nature of moral norms, the articulation of marriage, its sacramentality and indissolubility, all coalesce into a pastoral practice regarding marital failure and the remarriage of divorced Catholics.

In theological and canonical circles the approach to such people has undergone a significant evolution. Previously, there was one and only one response to someone who had contracted a church wedding: If you cannot keep the marriage together and if a church court does not grant an anulment, then you may live apart but never remarry. If someone acted contrary to that discipline and did remarry, but later sought to return to full participation in the life of the church, they were required to leave the invalid union. In those instances where such a separation would cause extreme harm, then a couple could be allowed to live together as "brother and sister."[25]

The first change that has occured is in the procedures and theory which guide the church tribunal system. Responding to the growing number of Catholics who have experienced a breakdown of their marriages, the theological and canonical tradition has developed so that more Catholics are able to have recourse to the external forum of church tribunals in order to find the freedom to remarry.[26]

But these developments were soon found to be inadequate to the complexity of the situation. What could be done for those who had been in a previous union that they believed to be invalid, but which for a variety of reasons could not be submitted to a tribunal? What of those who had been in a previous union they believed to be valid, but who now are in a second union that is permanent and stable? Is there no way in which they might return to the life of the church? In either or both of these situations, is there any way in which the couple could have some public recognition of this second union?

At the same time as these questions were being raised, a related issue was being debated: What is the relationship between full participation in the Eucharist and indissolubility? Is it possible for one who has celebrated a valid union where both parties are still alive, and is in a second union, to receive the Eucharist?

The discussion of these questions has been extensive, and it would be inappropriate to say that there is a clear theological consensus on all issues. It is possible to give an outline of what many would suggest is a "probable" opinion on certain of these questions and what, in fact, has become the pastoral practice in many parts of the church in the United States and which, in some local churches, exists with episcopal approval.[27]

First, there is a large number of theologians who hold that there is no necessary union between indissolubility and reception of the Eucharist. There are valid reasons to argue that in certain situations it is possible for one who is living in a second but irregular union to receive the sacraments. Once this has been determined as possible, then the question of "when" becomes foremost.[28]

Second, there is a recognition that the pastoral response to marital failure should recognize the different types of situations which are present. For those who in good conscience believe their previous union was invalid, should they not be allowed to share in the sacramental life of the church. The answer to this question for many is a rather firm yes. Because their problem cannot be solved in the external forum of the tribunal, it is proposed that an internal forum solution is possible. In this context of conscience and in light of certain general guidelines for the pastoral care of such situations, a return to full participation in the life of the church is possible. Such situations are described as "hardship" cases.[29]

While there appears to be a fair amount of theoretical and pastoral consensus on these cases, it is not as clear in the instance of one who knows that the previous union was valid. These situations are known as "conflict" cases, and some theologians would approve a cautious readmission to the sacraments on a case-by-case basis.[30]

There is even less consensus on whether there can be any kind of liturgical or para-liturgical recognition of these second unions. There has been no serious suggestion in print that such unions be regarded in the same manner as an external forum sacramental union. To do so would be to compromise the meaning of such unions. There has been discussion about, and in pastoral practice there have been attempts to provide, some kind of a celebration that while not being the same as a sacramental marriage would celebrate in an ecclesial and prayerful setting the goodness of the second union.[31]

The papal response to these developments continues the pattern which has emerged previously. There is a recognition of, and sensitivity to, the pastoral issues, but at the same time there is a firm disagreement over the response or resolution. The Holy Father recognizes that "Various reasons can unfortunately lead to the often irreparable breakdown of valid marriages (FC§83). He asks the ecclesial community to "support such people more than ever."

The document also recognizes that many Catholics who experience divorce "usually intend to enter a second union." Though calling this an evil, the pope says that the church "cannot abandon to their own devices those who have been previously bound by a sacramental marriage and who have attempted a second marriage" (FC§84). He goes on to say that pastors must carefully discern the situation because there is a difference between those who are suffering after having tried to save a marriage and those who, through their own fault, have destroyed a canonically valid marriage. In the spirit of this discernment, pastors and the whole community are called upon to help such people feel at home in the church and its life of prayer.

There are limits, however, to this participation. This is because "...the church reaffirms her practice, which is based upon sacred scripture, of not admitting to Eucharistic communion divorced people who have remarried" (FC§84). The reasons for this decision are two. First, the condition of the second union objectively violates the union which is signified by the Eucharist. Second, if this were to happen, "the faithful would be led into error and confusion regarding the church's teaching about the indissolubility of marriage" (FC§84). The only way possible for there to be participation in the sacramental life of the church would be for the couple to "take on themselves the duty to live in complete continence, that is, by abstinence from the acts proper to married couples" (FC§84).

For the same reasons, the pope says that it is forbidden for "...any pastor for whatever reason or pretext, even of a pastoral nature, to perform ceremonies of any kind for divorced people who remarry" (FC§84).

The full force of this discipline also would seem to apply to those who enter a second union and are "subjectively certain in conscience that their previous and irreparably destroyed marriage had never been valid" (FC§84).

With these words, the pope once again places himself at variance with a large number of theologians. While many theologians would be uncomfortable about suggesting that there is clarity on all of these issues, there would be a strong feeling that there have been enough historical, theological, and pastoral questions raised to suggest that there is need of a more nuanced reconsideration of the present discipline. The papal affirmation of the existing discipline with the firmness of its assertion would be considered premature and unfortunate.

Conclusion

The focus of these considerations has been a comparison of the theology of marriage found in the papal exhortation *Familiaris Consortio* and the manner in which some theologians are considering the same themes or topics. The results of the comparisons have been striking. It is obvious that the papal thought in many ways is similar to the thought of the theologians. This is especially true in what could be considered the more theoretical aspects of his thought. The pope acknowledges the theological significance of the "signs of the times," recognizes the diverse charisms within the ecclesial community, senses the complex nature of values and the need for growth in virtue, regards marriage as a community of life and love, affirms that sexuality is a dimension of the entire person, notes the need for adequate preparation within the journey of faith preparatory to marriage, and calls the church to a pastoral sensitivity towards those who experience marital failure.

Though there is this notable similarity or agreement, there is a striking disparity when it comes to the development and application of these concepts. The pope and theologians have very different postures on the role of the laity and theologians in discerning truth, on the meaning of moral norms, on the import of childbearing in marriage, on the nature of indissolubility, on the rejection of artificial birth control, and on denying access to the Eucharist for the divorced and remarried.

Such diversity in itself is not something to be feared. The life of the Christian community has seen such diversity throughout the centuries. What is disconcerting is the absence of the ways in which dialogue on these questions can be opened so that a consistent or integrated vision can be offered to the church. Three factors appear to be working against such a dialogue. First, there is the papal description of the role of the theologian. The theologians seem to be restricted to the explanation of what has already been decided. There is no clear theology of how the theologians may participate in the development of doctrine. Until there is agreement on this issue, there does not seem to be much opportunity for real dialogue.

Second, there is the almost dichotomous nature of the theology found in the exhortation. On the one hand, the pope seems to embrace the themes and values of the post-Vatican II enterprise. But, on the other hand, when those themes or values are brought to bear on more concrete or applied questions, the pope arrives at a very different set of conclusions than those of many theologians. It is not easy to discuss how such apparently common presuppositions can render such different conclusions.

Third, though the theologians have arrived at a different set of conclusions, most of them do so with a tentativeness that reflects a desire to reconcile the insights of the tradition with the results of contemporary thought and practice. The underlying assumption is that in areas of Christian practice, which are known to have been highly influenced by historical and cultural conditions, there is the possibility of change or development. The tenor of this exhortation, however, with its consistent reaffirmation of pastoral strategies which some would suggest have not been the perennial position of the church, appears to be opposed to such openness. If the implicit assumption of any conversation is that the mode of presentation can change but the conclusions cannot, then there is very little room for future dialogue.

Rather than being restricted by these factors which appear to complicate the possibility of dialogue, would it not be better for the theological community, in cooperation with the other sciences, to pursue those fundamental questions, the answers to which might provide the environment for a future conversation. Three such topics might be:

> What is the relationship between developing human experience and the meaning of the category "truth?" Can there be qualitative change in human understanding without losing any sense of objectivity or meaning?

> What is the meaning of human intimacy, its relationship to sexuality, procreation and marriage?

> What is the meaning of church? Is it a pilgrim community of sinners or an eschatological incarnation of divine ideals?

Hopefully, the good will of all and hard work of scholarship, combined with a great deal of patience, will insure that the dialogue takes place.

NOTES

1. For a description of the complexity of the contemporary theological enterprise, see the chapter entitled "The Pluralist Context of Contemporary Theology," in David Tracy's *Blessed Rage for Order* (New York: Seabury Press, 1975).

2. The Synod of Bishops is a post Vatican II development. In an attempt to express the collegial nature of the office of bishop and the intimate relationship between the college of bishops and bishop of Rome, the Synod of Bishops was established. It does not sit, however, as a legislative body. It meets at the summons of the pope, and it is not free to establish its own agenda. The results of its deliberations are advisory to the Holy See.

3. It is not possible to cite all of the material related to the activities of this Synod. A valuable resource is the NC Documentary Service *Origins*. Some pertinent material would be: the working paper prepared by the Synod Secretariat found in *Origins* 9 (1979) pp. 113-28; the working paper which was submitted to the Synod when it began its deliberations, found as excerpted in *Origins* (1980) pp. 227-33; various interventions of the Synod participants published during and after the Synod; and the Synod's final "Message to Christian Families" *Origins* 10 (1980) pp. 321-29.

4. For detailed references see: Edward Schillebeeckx, *Marriage: Human Reality, and Saving Mystery* (New York: Sheed and Ward, 1965); William Bassett and Peter Huizing, eds., *The Future of Christian Marriage*, Concilium, volume 87 (New York: Herder and Herder, 1973); Franz Bockle, ed., *The Future of Marriage as an Institution*, Concilium, volume 55 (New York: Herder and Herder, 1970); Charles E. Curran, "Divorce in Light of a Revised Moral Theology," *Ongoing Revision: Studies in Moral Theology* (Notre Dame: Fides, 1975), pp. 66-106; Charles E. Curran, "Divorce: Catholic Theory and Practice," *New Perspectives in Moral Theology* (Notre Dame: University of Notre Dame Press, 1976), pp. 212-76; Robert T. Kennedy and John T. Finnegan, "Select Bibliography on Divorce and Remarriage in the Church Today," *Ministering to Divorced Catholics*, James J. Young, ed., (New York: Paulist Press, 1979), pp. 260-76; Richard A. McCormick, "Notes on Moral Theology," *Theological Studies* 32 (1971) 107-22; 33 (1972) 91-100; 36 (1975) 100-117; and Seamus Ryan, "Surveys of Periodicals: Indissolubility of Marriage," *The Furrow* 24 (1973) 150-59, 214-24, 272-84, 356-74, 524-39. A more recent bibliography can be found in Thomas P. Doyle, O.P., ed., *Marriage Studies* (Toledo: Canon Law Society of America, 1980), pp. 78-101.

5. The selection of topics obviously reflects the theological interests of the writer. Several topics of significance are not considered both for want of space and lack of competence. Their exclusion is not a comment on their merit. In the same way, there is an obvious editorial judgment involved in the decision as to which theological positions will be presented. Without engaging in the impossible task of attempting to label the ideological postures that are presented, it is possible to say that these are the positions which a review of the recent proceedings of the Canon Law Society of America or of the Catholic Theological Society of America would find being discussed or cited.

6. For the development of the neo-Thomist paradigm, see Gerald McCool, *Catholic Theology in the Nineteenth Century* (New York: Seabury, 1977). This research and the work of other theologians has suggested that there have been a variety of ways in which the church has experienced itself. Various forces have contributed to these developments. For an analysis of these forces and an extended bibliography, see "A Social Portrait of the Theologian," in David Tracy, *The Analogical Imagination* (New York: Crossroad, 1981) pp. 3-46.

7. The best description of this position can be found in Bernard Lonergan's "The Transition from a Classicist World View to Historical Mindedness,"*Law for Liberty*, James Biechler, ed., (Baltimore: Helicon, 1967) pp. 126-33. The consequence of this model for the theological enterprise is developed by David Tracy in his revisionist model of theology. See Tracy, *Blessed Rage for Order*, pp. 43-64.

8. The ground-breaking work in this area of ecclesial models was that of Avery Dulles, *Models of the Church* (New York: Doubleday, 1974.) Similarly, Richard McBrien in his *Catholicism* (Minneapolis: Winston, 1980) pp. 691-728, develops his own notion of ecclesial models. The theological and historical sources of much of this work have been the writings of Yves Congar and Karl Rahner.

9. Avery Dulles summarizes this development when he says in his book, *Resilient Church* (Garden City: Doubleday, 1977), p. 100: "Among the living voices that have authority in the Church I would mention, in the first place, the general sense of the faithful. This is to be obtained not simply by counting noses but by weighing opinions. The views of alert and committed Christians should be given more weight than those of indifferent or marginal Christians, but even the doubts of marginal persons should be attentively considered to see if they do not contain some prophetic message for the Church. The sense of the faithful should be seen not simply as a static index but as a process. If it becomes clear that large numbers of generous, intelligent, prayerful, and committed Christians who seriously study a given problem change their views in a certain direction, this may be evidence that the Holy Spirit is so inclining them. But there is need for caution and discernment to avoid mistaking the influences of secular fashion for the inspirations of divine grace."
Intimately related to the role of the laity in the development of Catholic tradition is the question of dissent. For discussions of dissent from the magisterium see Richard McCormick in *Theological Studies* 29 (1968) pp. 714-18; 30 (1969) pp. 644-68; and 38 (1977) pp. 84-100; and in *Proceedings of the Catholic Theological Society of America* 24 (1969) pp. 239-54.

10. The relationship between the theologian and the magisterium has had a complex history. For a summary of a great deal of recent research, see *Chicago Studies* 17 (1978) which is devoted to the theme "The Magisterium, the Theologian and the Educator". The question of there being a "magisterium of doctors" is explored by Yves Congar, "Bref Histoire des Formes du 'Magistére' et ses relations avec les docteurs,"*Rev. des sciences phil. et theol.*, 60 (1976), p. 104. Also see Avery Dulles, S.J., "What is Magisterium?"*Origins* 6 (1976) pp. 81-87. For a recent commentary on the role of the moral theologian in the church, see Edward A. Malloy, C.S.C., "The Christian Ethicist in the Community of Faith,"*Theological* Studies 43 (1982) pp. 399-427.

11. For the teaching of Pius XII on the role of the theologian, see his encyclical *Humani Generis*, AAS 42 (1959) pp. 561 and 562.

12. Writers such as Curran, Dedek, O'Connell, Keane and McCormick would exemplify this approach.

13. The debate over the role of conflict and its consequences for the ethical enterprise has been central to Roman Catholic moral theology for almost twenty years. For a collection of some of the most important writings within the debate, see *Doing Evil to Achieve Good* edited by Richard McCormick and Paul Ramsey (Chicago: Loyola Press, 1978). To follow the history of this debate, the writings of McCormick in his annual "Moral Notes" in *Theological Studies* are an invaluable resource. Recently, fifteen years of his articles have been published in a collection entitled *Notes on Moral Theology, 1965 through 1980* (Washington, D.C.: University Press of America, 1981). For a systematic presentation of the theological posture

which incorporates a full recognition of the role of conflict, see Timothy O'Connell, *Principles for a Catholic Morality* (New York: Seabury Press, 1978).

14. This position is developed by O'Connell, *Principles*, pp. 83-97.

15. Though the question of compromise has been discussed by many others, it has been treated explicity by Charles Curran. For examples of his thought, see his *A New Look at Christian Morality* (Notre Dame: Fides, 1968) pp. 169-73, 232-33 and his *Catholic Moral Theology in Dialogue* (Notre Dame: University of Notre Dame Press, 1976) pp. 216-19. For a discussion of his theory, see my article "The Pastoral Implications of Charles Curran's Theory of Compromise," *Chicago Studies* 17 (1978) pp. 225-41.

16. Recently there has been a great deal of scholarly work on the history of, and theological developments surrounding, the Christian understanding of marriage. Inspired by Edward Schillebeeckx's *Marriage: Human Reality, Saving Mystery* (New York: Sheed and Ward, 1965), other theologians and historians have traced the development of the church's understanding of marriage. Two such recent works are Walter Kasper, *Theology of Christian Marriage* (New York: Seabury, 1980) and Theodore Mackin, S.J., *What is Marriage?* (New York: Paulist, 1982). For a popular review of the history of Christian marriage, see Michael D. Place, "The History of Christian Marriage," *Chicago Studies* 18 (1979) pp. 311-26. As a reference point, citations pertaining to the development of an understanding of marriage will be from Mackin. The impact of the middle ages can be found in Mackin's *What is Marriage?*, pp. 145-76.

17. Mackin, *What is Marriage?*, pp. 176-224.

18. The shift in perspective on the meaning of Christian marriage involved a major transition in Catholic thought. The acceptance of marriage as being covenantal in nature has had an effect on the theological and canonical life of the church. An overview of this movement can be found in Mackin, *What is Marriage?*, pp. 225-327. For a sampling of the theological journal writing on this subject and a fuller bibliography of some of the early writing on this question, see Paul F. Palmer, "Christian Marriage: Contract or Covenant," *Theological Studies* 33 (1974) pp. 617-65, and Mackin, "Conjugal Love and the Magisterium," *The Jurist* (1976) pp. 263-301. To understand how this change in perspective has affected the canonical tradition and the practices of the American tribunal system, as well as for an extensive bibliography on this subject, see Thomas P. Doyle, O.P., "Matrimonial Jurisprudence in the United States," *Marriage Studies* 2 (1982) pp. 111-59.

19. The literature on the question of the meaning of indissolubility and whether it is the best expression of the notion of marital permanence is vast. Certain works have contributed significantly to the dialogue. They are: Bernard Haring, "A Theological Appraisal of Marriage Tribunals," *Divorce and Remarriage in the Catholic Church*, Lawrence G. Wrenn, ed., (New York: Newman Press, 1973) pp. 18-21 and Lawrence G. Wrenn, "Marriage—Indissoluble or Fragile," in the same work, pp. 134-47. Also see Charles E. Curran, "Divorce: Catholic Theory and Practice," *New Perspectives in Moral Theology* (Notre Dame: University of Notre Dame Press, 1976) pp. 212-76 and Richard A. McCormick, "Indissolubility and the Right to the Eucharist: Separate Issues or One?" *Canon Law Society of America Proceedings* 37 (1975) pp. 26-37. For a review and commentary on this discussion, see McCormick, *Notes on Moral Theology* pp. 544-63.

20. For a brief overview of this approach to sexuality, see Philip S. Keane, S.S., *Sexual Morality, A Catholic Perspective* (New York: Paulist, 1977) pp. 5-13.

21. There are two works in English which exemplify this change in understanding. They are the work of Philip Keane cited in the note above and the controversial Anthony Kosnik,

et al., *Human Sexuality: New Directions in American Catholic Thought* (New York: Paulist, 1977). The literature surrounding the publication of *Human Sexuality* is extensive. For an initial survey, see McCormick, *Notes on Moral Theology*, pp. 737-45.

22. The historical setting of this understanding is found in Mackin, *What Makes Marriage*, pp. 145-224.

23. A sampling of the writing which has contributed to this new theology of marriage would include: Karl Rahner, "Marriage As a Sacrament," *Theological Investigations, Vol. 10* (New York: Herder and Herder (1973) pp. 199-221; Edward Killmartin, "When Is Marriage A Sacrament?" *Theological Studies* 34 (1973) pp. 275-86; William J. LaDue, "The Sacrament of Marriage," *Canon Law Society of America Proceedings* 36 (1974) pp. 25-35. A recent article by Ladislas Orsy, S. J., "Faith, Sacrament, Contract and Christian Marriage: Disputed Questions," *Theological Studies* 43 (1982) pp. 379-98 reviews the current state of the discussion and proposes a contemporary understanding of faith in his footnote 6.

24. For a description of this evolving pastoral practice and its complexity, see Orsy, "Christian Marriage: Disputed Questions" cited above and James A. Schmeiser, "Welcomed Civil Canonical Marriages," *Studia Canonica* 14 (1980) pp. 49-88; also Walter Cuenin, "The Marriage of Baptized Non-Believers," Origins 9 (1978) pp. 321-28. For one description of a program that prepares the Catholic couple for marriage, see *A Special Kind of Loving* (Chicago: Buckley, 1980) which summarizes the work of the Marriage and Family Life Office of the Archdiocese of Chicago.

25. For a summary of the previous discipline and the developments which have taken place in recent years, as well as a popular review of the subject matter of this section, see Thomas J. Green, "Canonical-Pastoral Reflection on Divorce and Remarriage," *Living Light* 13 (1976) pp. 560-76.

26. For extensive discussions on the present state of the law and tribunal practice as well as possible future changes resulting from the promulgation of a new Code, see Thomas J. Green: "The Revised Schema De Matrimonio: Text and Reflections," *The Jurist* 40 (1980) pp. 57-137; "Marriage Nullity Procedures in the Schema *De Processibus*," *The Jurist* 38 (1978) pp. 311-414, and "The Revision of the Procedural Law Schema: Implications for Tribunal Practice," *The Jurist* 40 (1980) pp. 349-83. All three of these articles contain excellent bibliographical references to the literature on the theology of marriage as well as the revision of church law and procedures.

27. Two articles which summarize much of the recent discussion are James H. Provost, "Intolerable Marriages Revisited," *The Jurist* 40 (1980) pp. 141-96 and Anthony Diacetis and Michael Place, "Alternative Possibilities for Pastoral Care for the Remarried." *Canon Law Society of America Proceedings* 43 (1981) pp. 270-84. Also see McCormick, *Moral Notes*, pp. 332-48, 372-80, 544-61, 826-40.

28. The most articulate statement of this position can be found in McCormick, "Indissolubility and the Right to the Eucharist."

29. A suggested set of guidelines for such hardship situations was proposed by a committee of the Canon Law Society of America (Committee on Alternatives to Tribunal Procedures, *Canon Law Society of America Proceedings* 37 (1975) pp. 170-74. They were: "(1) the previous marriage (or marriages) is irretrievably broken and reconciliation is impossible; (2) obligations incurred by virtue of the previous marriage are accepted and responsibly discharged; (3) obligations arising from the present union are accepted and responsibly discharged; (4) a willingness to live the Christian faith in the ecclesial community is apparent." For a study of the canonical implication of internal forum solutions, see Robert W. Thrasher,

"Reflections on Canon 1014," *Marriage Studies*, Thomas P. Doyle, ed. (Toledo: Canon Law Society of America, 1980). pp. 144-45. For a popular presentation of this matter and other related questions, see Thomas J. Green, "Ministering to Marital Failure," *Chicago Studies* 18 (1979) pp. 327-44.

30. The discussion of these two types of situations has not been confined to theological or canonical journals. For a review of discussions and actions taken by bishops and the Holy See, *see* Provost, "Intolerable Marriages Revisited," pp. 174-93.

31. One of the clearest discussions of this possibility can be found in Curran, "Divorce: Catholic Theory and Practice," pp. 246-47.

PART TWO

Family as the Basic Unit
of Society

Introduction

In a world haunted by the apocalypse, *Familiaris Consortio* calls for the family to be a source of love, compassion, and tolerance for its members and all of humanity.

> The family must help man to discern his own vocation and to accept responsibility in the search for greater justice, educating him from the beginning in interpersonal relationships, rich in justice and in love (FC§2).

It seems we need a source, a basic unit of society devoted and committed to fostering and nurturing what is best in us all. If the family does not or cannot perform this function, is there another institution that will? Certainly not business nor industry, which are focused on the maximization of profit often at the expense of competitors and the consumer. Certainly not government, which is preoccupied with negotiating and controlling the diverse interests of the nation. Can educational institutions serve as sources of justice and love when they must struggle with scarce resources while trying to teach children and young adults of widely different backgrounds? Will organized religion be our source of compassion, love, and justice, when religious groups tout their ideas of faith in the mass media and political arenas with the help of the latest marketing techniques?

If the family is not a center for expressing compassion for humanity, especially patience and care for children, we will not have such a center. If the family turns only inward, we may not have a political force reaching out to humanize our social institutions in the name of justice, kindness, and fellowship. *Familiaris Consortio* argues:

> Modern culture must be led to a more profoundly restored covenant with divine wisdom.... And it is only in faithfulness to this covenant that the families of today will be in a position to influence positively the building of a more just and fraternal world (FC§8).

The authors of the papers in this section address the problem of building a more just and fraternal world, and they make the following assumptions: (1) the family is the basic social unit responsible for nurturing its members and expressing to its fellows the wisdom of justice and love in the Judeo-Christian heritage; (2) although the family is affected by and in turn affects the larger community, it can and should be a miniature church acting as an evangelizing presence in the community; (3) social science is a means to better understand the conditions of contemporary life which assist or support the family as a humanizing presence in society.

Mary G. Durkin's paper, "Love and Intimacy: Revealing God in Family Relationships," develops the theme of the mystery of God's presence inherent in the expression of human intimacy. After a historical review of the Church's approach to human intimacy, Durkin examines the social science, theological, moral, and pastoral perspectives on marital intimacy in *Familiaris Consortio*. She relates the document's position on marital intimacy to the experience of marital intimacy in the modern world.

Charles and Mary Ellen Wilber's paper, "The Economy, the Family, and Social Justice," develops the theme of the family as a communion of love reaching out to humanize the neighborhood, the community, and the larger society.

Stanley Saxton and Michael Katovich seek to identify the nature of "rich" interpersonal relationships. *Familiaris Consortio* calls for the family to be a community of selflessness and tolerance, a communion of persons rich with love which cradles the next generation of human beings within the family. It is society at its best in miniature form.

4

Love and Intimacy

Revealing God in Family Relationships

Mary G. Durkin, D.Min.

In a recent interview Helen Gurly Brown, the guru of *Cosmopolitan Magazine*, recommended affairs as the best way to really get to know someone. She also endorsed affairs with married men as the only solution for the problems women confront because there are not enough men to go around. Most of us are familiar with the consequences this modern form of "polygamy" causes for the "other woman." Recent publicity connected with palimony trials reinforces the belief that this sort of relationship is not as uncomplicated as Ms. Brown seems to indicate. So, too, newspapers are filled with reports of problems encountered in the area of intimacy. Magazine articles and books abound with advice on how to be intimate, advice which is considered a sure-fire selling tool for their publications. All this would lead us to suggest that we humans are in a crisis of intimacy. The apostolic exhortation, *Familiaris Consortio*, seems to have this crisis in mind when it speaks of the negative aspects of the situation of the family in the world. Our analysis of love and intimacy in light of the ideas presented in *Familiaris Consortio* will seek to discern how the exhortation addresses this problem.

A basic presupposition of this paper is that human intimacy, especially marital intimacy, has been, is now, and probably always will be, an experience that exposes us to 'mystery'. Before analyzing the response of *Familiaris Consortio* to this experience of mystery, we will present a consideration of the role of religious imagination as a link between the experience of mystery and the God of our religious tradition. This will provide us with a tool for evaluating the discussion of love and intimacy in the apostolic exhortation. In our conclusion we will offer some recommendations for further research that might provide ideas on how to incorporate the exhortation's positive ideas on intimacy into the ongoing life of the Church.

51

RELIGIOUS IMAGINATION AND MARITAL INTIMACY

There has been in the past, and there continues to be, a strong link between a religious understanding of the meaning of life and the way in which humans respond to the powerful sexual attraction of man for woman and woman for man. In the past this link was more explicit than it is today. At the present time the connection between what one believes to be ultimate in life and how one responds to one's sex drive is not always apparent.

Religious traditions, including the Roman Catholic tradition, which prescribed specific rules for correct sexual and marital behavior based on interpretations of Divine Law, often failed to encourage the development of love in marital relationships. Today, if these religious traditions want to speak to the experience of marital intimacy in the modern world, they are faced with the task of reevaluating their understanding of marital intimacy in light of the tradition's understanding of the ultimate meaning of life. This is not a call to tie the tradition's understanding of God to the experiences of a particular culture. Rather it sees religious tradition operating as a transformer of a culture, calling the culture to its highest possibility.

When the Church's official stand on marriage and sexuality remains closely linked with previous cultures, it becomes difficult, in the absence of any reinterpretation, for that stand to speak to a different culture experience. For a reinterpretation of the Christian perspective on marriage to be effective for the modern world, it is necessary to understand how religion operates in people's lives.

For most of the history of Christianity there was a separation between the elites of the Church who could read and write and were concerned about doctrine and moral law and the ordinary lay person whose commitment to the Church was often the result of stories of faith passed on from previous generations. People in that period of human history paid scant attention to nuanced theological discussions. In the counter-Reformation mentality of the fortress Church of the more recent past, the laity and the heirarchy based membership in the Catholic Church on a person's ability to adhere to a sexual and a marital morality that were considered absolute and unchangeable components of the Catholic faith, enshrined from the very beginning in the exact form they took in the twentieth century.

In the post-Vatican II Church, a new understanding of the role of religion has evolved. Though not all church leaders are aware of this evolution, or if aware are willing to accept its validity, the fact remains that there exist two, at times opposed, perspectives on how religion operates in people's lives. The "from above" perspective of many church authorities sees religion as rooted in creeds, theology, and moral statements guarded by the Church and interpreted for the ordinary people, whose membership in the Church depends on their acceptance of the magisterium's interpretation. The other perspective sees religion as a power that arises from the lives of the people themselves—from the encounter with mystery in the ordinary and extraordinary experiences of human living. This perspective sees grace abounding in the experiences of people's lives, waiting for them to be aware of this Divine Presence and to begin a search for a better appreciation of it.

In this second perspective, creeds, theology, morality, and church authority are seen as transforming vehicles, as helps for linking the encounter with mystery in everyday experience with the understanding of the meaning of life found in the biblical tradition. The transformative power of these church vehicles becomes operative, not through rules and regulations but through an ability to spark the religious imagination of the faithful.

Sociological research and theological reflection have deepened our appreciation of the influence of the creative imagination on religious attitudes, values, and behaviors. People's lives are affected not so much by creed, doctrines, and morality statements as they are by the way in which the stories of faith, which encapsulate and flesh out the intellectual content of abstract statements, speak to experiences in their lives. For example, even though the fortress mentality of the counter-Reformation Church required acceptance of the indissolubility of marriage for membership in that Church, the law of indissolubility did not on its own assure the sacramentality of marital relationships. The woman who was "faithful" for more than fifty years of a marriage but who on her forty-eighth anniversary bitterly said to her daughter, "Forty-eight years to the wrong man," stayed married because the Church taught "until death do us part." However, she was never challenged to discover the religious dimension of marital intimacy uncovered in the various stories of our faith. Neither she nor her spouse were ever encouraged to grow in psychological and sexual intimacy so their faithfulness might be sacramental, a reflection of Divine Love.

If the Church recognizes the importance of sparking the religious imagination, it does not abandon theology, creeds, and reflections on morality; rather it seeks to mine both the richness of its theological and moral tradition *and* the richness of the experience of God in people's lives. In this perspective religious leaders are seen as those who form links and build bridges between the tradition and experience. They must be about the task of uncovering a spirituality that will inspire people to transform the experiences of their lives in light of the God of the religious tradition.

In the pluralistic society of our modern technological culture where people are experiencing the paradoxical nature of the call to marital intimacy, a religious tradition will be able to influence the attitudes, values, and behaviors of its adherents when it challenges them to an integrated understanding of marital intimacy; that is, when it presents a vision of marital intimacy that links the social, psychological, and sexual dimensions of intimacy with a religious understanding of the meaning of life. This approach recognizes the importance of the social and psychological implications of the powerful human sexual drive and, at the same time, recognizes that there is both a potential for good and a potential for evil in this drive. A religious vision encourages us to choose the positive potential rather than the demonic. Religion will assist marital partners on the journey of marital intimacy when it inspires them to new growth and development, helping them to move beyond the inevitable crises which occur in any attempt to share identity in a depth relationship. Spouses need to be inspired; they need to be "enspirited"; they need to be encouraged in their search for the good, the true, and the beautiful, in their journey toward God.

INTIMACY IN *FAMILIARIS CONSORTIO*

Bishop J. Francis Stafford told a group of theologians who were examining the apostolic exhortation that the document reflects "fully and accurately" the mind of the bishops who participated in the synod. The recommendation of the synod delegates to the Holy Father had been considered, he was sure, in compilation of the apostolic exhortation. Concerns of bishops throughout the world were contained in those recommendations, resulting in a document for the whole world which might require interpretation when applied to specific situations.

The issue of marital intimacy as a journey in the growth and development of love is addressed in a variety of ways in the apostolic exhortation, often implicitly rather than explicitly. In order to evaluate the document's contribution to a discussion of marital intimacy, it will be helpful to consider the various disciplinary understandings of marital intimacy reflected in the document, even though these are not always explicitly identified. We will evaluate the ideas which are implied in the statement in light of how they might provide inspiration to a religious imagination confronted with the paradoxical nature of the quest for marital intimacy. This thematic approach is imposed on the document making both overlap and contradictions obvious.

The task of applying the ideas on marital intimacy in *Familiaris Consortio* to the American situation requires that we be aware of the implicit and explicit social science, theological, moral, and pastoral perspectives present in the document. This approach will supply us with a basis for developing suggestions for further study of the relationship between marital intimacy and the Catholic Christian tradition.

Social Science Perspective

In order to evaluate how effectively the apostolic exhortation speaks to the paradoxical nature of the quest for human intimacy in the modern world, it is necessary to uncover the understanding of human intimacy underlying the exhortation's reflections. Explicitly, the document acknowledges the role of sociological and statistical research as one factor which is "helpful in understanding the historical context in which pastoral action has to be developed" (FC§5). The document also calls for more detailed study of the process of "inculturation" (FC§10). Specifically, regarding intimacy, there is a call for investigation of the causes of "trial marriages" including their "psychological and sociological aspect in order to find the proper remedy" (FC§79). At the same time the different human sciences are encouraged "to study further *the difference, both anthropological and moral,* between contraception and recourse to the rhythm of the cycle" (FC§32); thus, the document explicitly recognizes the contribution the social sciences can make to an understanding of marriage and the family, though there is a caution against allowing the results of social science research to be sole criterion of correct moral behavior (FC§5).

In addition, certain passages within the document indicate an implicit acceptance of the findings of research in the social sciences. The section on the changing roles of men and women responds to many of the work/home related issues confronting families in a technological culture (FC§§22-25). The implications of these changes for the initial commitment over an extended period of time is not specifically touched upon.

The treatment of the societal dimension of marital intimacy, especially as intimacy serves to model values for the next generation, implicitly acknowledges psychological and sociological research in values transmission. Remote preparation for marriage takes place in childhood, "the period when esteem for all authentic human values is instilled both in interpersonal and social relationships" (FC§66); this preparation is strongly influenced by the intimacy relationship of the parents which affects much of adult religious behavior.

The call for fidelity to the commitment of marital intimacy as a help to growth and development in the relationship (FC§19), as well as the emphasis on love as the principle and power of communion in the relationship of marriage (FC§18), and the recognition that there are trials and difficulties in every relationship (FC§§ 20,58) show some recognition of both the importance and the difficulty of emotional bonding in an intimacy relationship. Still, we do not find the analysis of the "historical situation in which the family lives" acknowledging both the problems and the possibilities encountered in a search for intimacy now that there is an increased life span and lower infant mortality rates.

Also, though there are some references to an anthropological understanding of the family, the implications of an evolutionary perspective on human sexuality and marital intimacy are not specifically addressed. The interplay between the sexual, psychological, and social dimensions of marital intimacy is not acknowledged. Indeed, much of the attention to sexual intimacy is linked to its reproductive possibilities, leading us to wonder if the agenda of previous cultures and their interests are not active here.

For example, there is no specific reference to sexual intimacy during the long period of a marital relationship when the wife's menopause completely rules out procreation. The only reference to physical sterility seems to be addressed to instances of marriage during the normal reproductive years (FC §14).

The document's focus on the reproductive aspects of sexual intimacy (FC §§29-35) along with its call for continence on the part of divorced and remarried Catholics who wish to participate in the Eucharist (FC §84) fails to take into consideration the bonding aspects of sexual intimacy. In the case of the heavy emphasis on the reproductive possibilities of sexual intimacy, the document fails to underline the importance of the bonding capabilities. In the instance of the prohibition against the reception of the Eucharist for divorced and remarried Catholics who do not practice total continence, the document ignores the importance of sexual intimacy for parents who want to model Divine Love for the children of such a union.

These are just some of the observations which we find in the document relevant to the possibilities for intimacy in the modern world. Evaluating these observations in light of the social science understanding of the journey of marital intimacy in a technological culture, we find instances where the fruits of this research are obvious and other instances where it is not even considered.

Theological Perspective

The theological perspective we find articulated in the various segments of *Familiaris Consortio* speaks to the issue of marital intimacy by drawing on some of the most basic doctrines of the Catholic tradition. We find a summary of this in the introduction:

Willed by God in the very act of creation, marriage and the family are interiorly ordained to fulfillment in Christ and have need of His graces in order to be healed from the wounds of sin and restored to their "beginning"; that is, to the full understanding and the full realization of God's plan (FC§3).

Later, we read how love, including the human body as a sharer in spiritual love, is the "fundamental and innate vocation of every human being" as the result of our creation in God's image and likeness. Also, sexual intimacy, which is not purely biological but concerns the innermost being of the human person, is seen as truly human only if it is an integral part of the love of total commitment made possible by marriage (FC§11). There is, it seems, a possibility for marital intimacy because of the Divine Gift of Creation. Redemption by Christ and our participation in that redemption calls for:

> Conjugal love [that] involves a totality, in which all the elements of the person enter—appeal of the body and instinct, power of feeling and affectivity, aspiration of the spirit and of will. It aims at a deeply personal unity, the unity that, beyond union in one flesh, leads to the forming of one heart and soul; it demands indissolubility and faithfulness in definitive mutual giving; and it is open to fertility (FC§13).

The presentation of the family as a sharer of the mystery of the church carrying on the role of Jesus Christ as Prophet, Priest, and King points the way to an understanding of the religious and sacramental dimensions of marital intimacy (FC§§49-64). The importance of the Eucharist and Christian penance in assisting in the growth of marital intimacy relates the doctrine of the Holy Spirit to the ongoing quest for marital intimacy (FC§§56-58). The call to love not only each other but to share this love beyond the couple in the family (FC§63) even to influencing the church to "take on a more homelike or family dimension, developing a more human and fraternal style of relationships" (FC§64) highlights the transformative power of the intimacy relationship when spouses are journeying together in a search for Divine Love.

The theology of intimacy, often only implicitly present in this document but more explicitly developed in the series of papal audience addresses designed to accompany the synod preparations "from afar," indicates that there is a powerful storehouse of visionary potential in our religious tradition relevant to the quest for marital intimacy. The implications of this vision for the situation of marital intimacy need to be explored more fully than they are in this exhortation.

Morality Perspective

The values, attitudes, and behaviors that flow from an interaction between an analysis of a situation and the basic beliefs of a religious tradition give us the basis for a morality perspective regarding that situation. In the instance of marital intimacy in the apostolic exhortation, there are specific morality injunctions, some of which flow from the interaction between the situation and the faith tradition, while others seem more relevant to previous historical periods. This causes some difficulty, especially if we want the faith tradition to enspirit those who participate in the journey of marital intimacy in the modern world.

Morality statements need to be related to the experiences of people's lives if they are to be helpful in decisions regarding correct behavior. Even if the statements are a negative judgment on people's experiences, they must be related to these experiences as they occur if people are to find the judgments relevant. The basic principles enunciated in the Charter of Family Rights regarding "the right to intimacy of conjugal and family life and the right to the stability of the bond and of the institution of marriage"(FC §46) along with the other rights of the family are principles which all of us could see as flowing from the interaction of the contemporary situation and our religious tradition.

Some of the more specific morality statements cause difficulty for us when they seem to ignore the reality of the situation of marital intimacy in contemporary experience. This is especially true in the statements on the indissolubility of marriage and the statements on contraception.

One of the main difficulties with the document's treatment of the indissolubility of marriage is not with the argument that fidelity is an important component in a marital union but with the lack of acknowledgement of the facts of the situation of marital intimacy in the modern world. Mistakes in the choice of a marital partner can and do interfere with the sacramental possibilities of a marital union, a fact acknowledged by the church's policy on annulment. The dilemma of psychological incompatibility in a marital union which could last for fifty years does serve as the basis for church annulments but simply is not acknowledged here. For people in a country where annulments have been on the increase (not a universal church phenomenon, however) this causes skepticism regarding the document.

So, too, does the claim for an anthropological and moral difference between contraception and recourse to the rhythm of the cycle (FC§32) and the claim that contraception contradicts the total reciprocal self-giving of husband and wife and "leads not only to a positive refusal to be open to life but also to a falsification of the inner truth of conjugal love...(FC§32)."

They do not seem to relate to the actual experiences of many people. Some people find it difficult to believe that the document's discussion of sexual intimacy, contraceptive mentality (which could sometimes be a motive for people using the rhythm of the cycle and not necessarily a motive for those using another form of contraception), and the aesthetical practice of periodic continence simply does not take into consideration the interplay between the sexual, social, psychological, and religious dimensions of marital intimacy as they are experienced in the day-to-day living of marriage and family life.

While there are certainly dangers in the use of contraception, the reasons presented in the document are not convincing for many people. While everyone would agree that there is a need for dialogue, reciprocal respect, shared responsibility, and self-control in the search for sexual intimacy, many spouses would admit they need encouragement to discover the grace possibilities present in a nurturing of their sexual attraction, and they see too much control of passion in their intimacy relationships.

In order for the theological perspective which values fidelity and new life to be influential in guiding moral behavior, it must discover a way to encourage people to avoid the dangers of infidelity and the contraceptive mentality. Thus far church authority and moral pronouncements have been ineffective.

Pastoral Perspective

The church which "accompanies the Christian family on its journey through life" (FC§65) wishes to assist couples in their search for marital intimacy. This document spells out some ways in which pastoral activity might help people to make the journey of marital intimacy be a journey toward God. To this end there are recommendations for remote, proximate, and immediate preparation for marriage which recognize the importance of all three stages of preparation. The exhortation also recognizes the freedom of people to marry and, except under the most extenuating circumstances, the need to celebrate their marriage within the church (FC§§66-68). This is an important consideration which emphasizes the religious dimension of marital intimacy. So too, the call for pastoral care after marriage (FC§69) recognizes the cyclical nature of marital intimacy and the specific problems at various stages of married life. The pastoral perspective found in this concluding section recognizes the integrating nature of the religious dimension of marital intimacy as it challenges people to face the paradoxes encountered in the other dimensions. In this way the document sets the stage for church emphasis on the importance of the religious dimension.

This review of the four perspectives found in *Familiaris Consortio* uncovers the positive ideas which could contribute to an enrichment of the experience of marital intimacy and, at the same time, highlights some difficulties that could be encountered in relating this document to the experience of marital intimacy in the modern world. This leads us to conclude that the translation of this documet to the specific experience of marital intimacy in the North American experience requires collaboration between scholars and pastoral workers.

PASTORAL AND SCHOLARLY RESPONSE

The previous evaluation of the apostolic exhortation's treatment of love and marital intimacy leads us to the conclusion that the application of its positive insights into a theology of marital intimacy requires a more precise linking of the experience of marital intimacy and the beliefs of our Catholic tradition. This requires additional study of the experience of marital intimacy by social and biological scientists and further theological reflection by systematic and pastoral theologians. Such study will be most fruitful when done in an interdisciplinary context. For this reason, centers such as the Center for the Study of Family Development at the University of Dayton are needed to encourage interdisciplinary discussions that will lead to a deeper understanding of the experience of marital intimacy and a relating of the transformative possibilities of the religious tradition for this experience. Theologians, both systematic and pastoral, need to be aware of the various aspects of marital intimacy. In the theologians' role as advisors to the magisterium of the church they must make this information available to the hierarchy.

Some specific areas of collaborative research become apparent in light of our reflections on marital intimacy and on the theological view that marital intimacy is a revelation of Divine Love, bestowed as a gift in the act of creation. These are:

1. A more detailed analysis of the interaction of the various dimensions of marital intimacy is crucial. Catholic scholars need to apply the fruits of research in their individual fields to the development of this integrated view. When necessary, they should undertake research in those areas which we do not presently understand.

2. We need a deeper understanding of how the religious tradition influences the ongoing experience of people's lives and how it specif-

ically can influence the journey of marital intimacy. Issues such as religious imagination, spirituality, the influence of moral statements, the transmission of values, and possibilities for educational and other support activities need to be studied.

3. Theologians must be about the task of applying the transformative vision of our faith tradition to the experience of marriage. Pastoral theologians must interact with academic theologians presenting the latter with the paradoxical nature of marital initmacy and gaining from them a fuller insight into the richness of the religious tradition.

4. A means for communication between pastoral workers at all levels—parish, diocese, national conference, and the universal church—including laity, religious clerics, heirarchy, and scholars is of paramount importance for the study of the experience of marital intimacy.

5. The "elites" of the church, be they lay, religious, clerics, bishops, or scholars, must not lose sight of the importance of the religious tradition as a support for people grappling with the paradox of their search for marital intimacy. At the same time, the "elites" must understand that as a result of the grace of creation and the grace of redemption, the experience of marital intimacy has the capacity for revealing God. This capacity should not be ignored.

If marital intimacy is a sign of "the unfailing fidelity with which God and Jesus Christ love each other and every human being" (FC§20) and if the love between husband and wife leads the family to a deeper and more intense *communion* which is the foundation and soul of the *community* of "marriage and the family" (FC§18), then we need a better understanding of the lived experience of marital intimacy. We need this not only in its abstract manifestation revealed through research, but we also need it in the ongoing experience of various individuals and groups. Only then will we begin to appreciate this dimension of God's revelation in our modern world.

5

The Economy, the Family, and Social Justice

Charles K. Wilber
Mary Ellen Wilber

UNIVERSITY OF NOTRE DAME
NOTRE DAME, INDIANA

Pope John Paul II's apostolic exhortation *Familiaris Consortio* (On the Family) appears at a most appropriate time. Developments in the economy have undermined the role of the family just when that role is more vital than ever. This paper argues that the family, as the key "mediating institution" in society, is needed as a prime agent of social justice in the economy.

INSTITUTIONAL CHANGE IN THE ECONOMY

United States society today is characterized by large corporations, unions, and government institutions. To cite just a few examples: In 1978 General Motors, Exxon, AT&T, and Ford Motor Company each had net sales larger than the GNP of over 120 countries. In 1978 the 200 largest manufacturing corporations held 62 percent of all manufacturing assets in the United States. And this is not all. Unions have matched the growth of industry. The Teamsters, UAW, and the Carpenters Union are all mega-institutions. Government agencies such as the Department of Defense are even larger. Socialist economies share this characteristic. Their economic institutions are even larger and more bureaucratized than our own.

The development of the United States economy (and most other industrialized economies) has created a fundamental dichotomization of social, political, and economic life.[1] Put most simply, the dichotomy is between the mega-institutions and the private life of the individual. These two divisions of our society are experienced and apprehended by the individual in quite different ways. As Peter Berger points out, the GMs, UAWs, DODs, UCLAs, and AMAs are "remote, often hard to understand or downright unreal, impersonal, and ipso facto unsatisfactory as sources for individual meaning and identity...By contrast, private life is experienced as the single most important area for the discovery and actualization of meaning and identity."[2]

People could cope with these mega-institutions if the dichotomization process had not so de-institutionalized the private lives of individuals. People have always found their identity and, in turn, impressed their values on the mega-institutions through what Berger calls "mediating structures." However, this interlocking network of mediating institutions—family, church, voluntary association, neighborhood, and subculture—has been severely weakened by the growth of the mega-institutions. These have taken over many of the traditional functions of the mediating institutions.

In the face of this dichotomization of modern life, the concept of Christian responsibility or stewardship falls on infertile soil. There are a number of reasons why this is true.

People feel helpless in the face of these mega-institutions. Their sheer size is so alienating that the individual retreats to private life believing that nothing can be done about *them* out there. However, private life is becoming less of a refuge as mediating institutions continue to decay in the face of the expansion of the mega-institutions. As Berger says, "The situation becomes intolerable...when, say, my wife leaves me, my children take on life styles that are strange and unacceptable to me, my church becomes incomprehensible, my neighborhood becomes a place of danger, and so on."[3] The result is a turn to hedonism and me-firstism at the worst and quietism at the best. And, of course, this further weakens the mediating institutions of private life.

Not only do people *feel* helpless to change this, but in fact they *are* helpless as individuals to make any difference. With the mega-institutions "taking care" of the hungry, the thirsty, the stranger, the naked, the ill, and the prisoner; and with the family, church, voluntary association, neighborhood, and subculture weakened and defensive, the individual finds it difficult if not impossible to carry out his or her Christian responsibilities for social justice.

A third factor is vital for understanding why the environment of modern life is alien to the practice of Christian stewardship and deserves extended treatment. As Berger says, "No society, modern or otherwise, can survive without what Durkheim called a 'collective conscience,' that is without moral values that have general authority."[4] Most economists have forgotten (if they ever knew) that Adam Smith said the same thing. While in *The Wealth of Nations*[5] he stressed the importance of competition (and assumed the small scale of institutions); in another, less well-known book,[6] he argued that widespread acceptance of a "general moral law" was a prerequisite for the proper functioning of the economy and society.

The assumption that individual self-interest in a competitive environment is sufficient to yield the common good is an illusion. An economy, capitalist or socialist, in which everyone—buyers, sellers, workers, managers, consumers, and firms—constantly lied, stole, committed fraud and violence, etc., would neither yield the common good nor would it be stable. Yet pushed to its logical extreme, individual self-interest often suggests that it is in the interest of an individual to evade the rules by which others are guided. Similarly, the "free-rider" concept suggests that it is in an individual's interest not to cooperate in a situation of social interdependence if others do cooperate, for he/she will obtain the same benefits without any sacrifice. Therefore, why do individuals in societies usually not operate in this fashion? The answer is not fear of the police but rather that our basic selfishness is inhibited by a deeply ingrained moral sense, one usually based on religious convictions.

Fred Hirsch reintroduces the idea of moral law into economic analysis: "truth, trust, acceptance, restraint, obligation—these are among the social virtues grounded in religious belief which...play a central role in the functioning of an individualistic, contractual economy... The point is that conventional, mutual standards of honesty and trust are public goods that are necessary inputs for much of economic output."[7]

The major source of this collective conscience or moral law has been the religious heritage of the precapitalist and preindustrial past, embodied as it was in the mediating institutions of private life. This legacy of religious values has diminished over time because of a two-fold change: (1) the repudiation of the social character and responsibility of religion meant its banishment to a purely private matter[8] and (2) the elevation of self-interest as a praiseworthy virtue in turn undermined that privatized religious ethic.

The erosion of this preindustrial, precapitalist moral legacy has proceeded slowly for two reasons: (1) economic growth was spread over a very long period and (2) that growth relied on decentralized decision making for the most part. This slow and seemingly natural process allowed popular acceptance of the social changes as well as permitted adjustment in the moral base of society. However, the limits to this process are now being reached in the United States.

Capitalist development was far from conflict-free in the past. But one of its advantages was the absence of an identifiable villain behind the disruptions that occured. Such changes resulted from the independent decisions of thousands of persons. Few could rig the rules to his or her benefit, so inequalities appeared legitimate and the undermining of religious values had no identifiable cause. The centrality of government in most developed countries today, however, provides a target for dissatisfaction. In such circumstances the legitimacy of inequalities and changes in values are open to question and to challenge. The gradual disappearance of the moral base of society forces government to attempt to act as a substitute and to provide a context which will encourage principled action among the elite while at the same time ensuring acceptance of the outcome by the majority. Thus, government must create, or in some sense embody, a "civil religion."

Let us summarize the argument thus far. The erosion of the inherited moral base under the onslaught of continuous growth and spread of individualism creates the following condition: The (entrepreneurial) elite and many other groups have been freed of the old religious and moral values, but the individualistic growth process has not provided any substitute social morality. Thus the previously effective inhibitions on lying, cheating, and stealing have lost their power and the functioning of the private sector is suffering as a result.

A second problem arises in the central role played by the state in managing the economy. There is a central flaw in the current approach of planned capitalist growth. It calls for the pursuit of self-interest by individuals in the private sector but forbids it in the public sector. The expectation that public servants will not promote their private interests at the expense of the public interest reinforces the argument that the economy rests just as much on moral behavior as it does on self-interest behavior. "The more a market economy is subjected to state intervention and correction, the more dependent its functioning becomes on restriction of the individualistic calculus in certain spheres, as well as on certain elemental moral standards among both the controllers and the controlled. The most important of these are standards of truth, honesty, physical restraint, and respect for law."[9] But the more that self-interest progresses and the more that the original moral base of society is undercut, the less likely are these conditions to be met.

Attempts to rely solely on material incentives in the private sector and more particularly in the public sector suffer from two defects: (1) to have a policeman on every corner to prevent cheating simply doesn't work. Regulators have less relevant information compared to those whose behavior they are trying to regulate. In addition, who regulates the regulators? Thus, there is no substitute for an internalized moral law that directs persons to seek their self-interest only in "fair" ways.[10] (2) A reliance on external sanctions further undermines the remaining aspects of an internalized moral law. Thus, the erosion of society's moral base under the onslaught of self-interest has important practical results.

Because of their remoteness and their sheer size, the mega-institutions are "consumers" not "producers" of such a general morality. As Berger
points out, "Bureaucrats are the poorest of *moralistes.*"[11] A general moral
code cannot rest on the activities of individuals either. The widespread
experiments with "lifestyles" of "consenting adults" is too unstable and un-
reliable a basis for the maintenance of a collective conscience. However,
without a collective conscience, the ethic of Christian stewardship must
languish.

CHANGES IN MORAL THEOLOGY

The dichotomization of modern life has been paralled by developments in moral theology. Two opposite but complementary phenomena are
important in this context, and are directly related to the Roman Catholic
tradition.

First is the shift of emphasis from personal to institutional sinfulness.
It is true that the previous focus on personal sins of commission obscured
the nature of systemic evil and the analogy that we put bandaids on cancers
is powerful. However, the present focus on institutional and systemic evil
undermines personal responsibility. Given the earlier point that mediating
institutions have been weakened severely and faced with the systemic evil
of the mega-institutions, a feeling of impotence overwhelms the individual.
Since there are few avenues for exercising personal responsibility, the con-
scientious individual ends up feeling guilty. And unrelieved guilt leads to
apathy or cynicism, which reinforces the dichotomization of life and further
undermines the prospects for Christian responsibility.

A second development in religious thought is the neglect of traditional
Catholic social teaching with its emphasis on subsidiarity;[12] that is, the
principle that tasks should be performed at the lowest possible level, beginning with the individual, and move upward through intermediate institutions to the national or global level as required. Instead, contemporary
Catholic social thought has mirrored the secular world's neglect of mediating institutions in favor of state action or individual social ministry. Thus,
the family, parish, and neighborhood have been on the defensive even
within religious social thought.

None of the above observations are meant to deny the importance of
recognizing institutional and systemic evil. Rather they are a call to see the
importance of mediating institutions—particularly the family—in providing the base for Christian stewardship to flourish and function as the means
of reforming societal structures.

THE ROLE OF MEDIATING INSTITUTIONS

Our modern political philosophies—liberalism, conservatism, and socialism—have failed up to now because they have not understood the importance of mediating institutions. Liberalism has constantly turned to the state and conservatism to the corporate sector for solutions to social problems. Neither recognizes the destructiveness to the social fabric which is caused by relying on mega-institutions. Socialism also suffers from this myopia. Even though it places its faith in renewed community, it fails to see that socialist mega-institutions are just as destructive as capitalist ones.

If we accept the importance of mediating institutions, there are two areas of concern. The first is that of public policy. For our present concerns we will merely cite our agreement with Peter Berger's two points: "One: *Public policy should protect and foster mediating structures.* Two: *Wherever possible, public policy should utilize the mediating structures as its agents.*"[13]

More importantly, ways must be found to revitalize mediating institutions from the bottom up. For the rest of this paper we will focus on the family as a key mediating institution. It is worthwhile to begin with a quote from *Familiaris Consortio*:

> ...society should never fail in its fundamental task of respecting and fostering the family.
>
> The family and society have complementary functions in defending and fostering the good of each and every human being. But society—more specifically the state—must recognize that "the family is a society in its own original right," and so society is under a grave obligation in its relations with the family to adhere to the principle of subsidiarity (FC§45).

The modern economy with its high level of occupational and geographic mobility, its sharp division of work life from home life, and its transfer of education, welfare, and old age security functions to mega-institutions has transformed the nature of the family. As a result *individual* families have difficulty coping with the dichotomization of modern life. Families can be a powerful force for Christian stewardship but they need help. Somehow individual families must band together in groups that can provide their members with an understanding of the social world, a mechanism for acting as Christians, and a faith that will permeate the other institutions of society.

In Latin America the *Comunidades de Base*[14] are functioning as mediating institutions for individuals and families. In Sri Lanka the *Sarvodaya Shramadana* movement is based on groups of families at the village level. Both the United States and Europe lack equivalent movements. The closest type of institution has been those built on Catholic action—Young Christian Students, Young Christian Workers, and the Christian Family Movement. All three are past their peak, but the basic philosophy has potential for revitalization in new structures. This is what the *Sarvodaya Shramadana* movement did with Buddhist values in Sri Lanka.

THE FAMILY AS A MEDIATING INSTITUTION

We want to deal with the role of the Christian family as a mediating institution within the people of God—"its own special gift, its own special grace, its special duty,"[15] and the way it functions as a mediating institution in society.

The Second Vatican Council sets out a social role for the Christian family which is extremely demanding. In addition to the raising of children as Christians, it calls for: "the adoption of abandoned infants, hospitality to strangers, assistance in the operating of schools, advice and help for adolescents, help to engaged couples, catechetical work, support of married couples and families in material or moral crises, help for the aged..."[16] And that is not all: "It is of the highest importance that families should devote themselves directly and by common agreement to transforming the very structure of society."[17]

Pope John Paul II reaffirms and extends the role of the family in *Familiaris Consortio*:

Families..., either singly or in association, can and should devote themselves to manifold social service activities, especially in favor of the poor or at any rate for the benefit of all peoples and situations that cannot be reached by the public authorities' welfare organization.

The social role of families is called upon to find expression also in the form of political intervention...

The Christian family is...called upon to offer everyone a witness of generous and disinterested dedication to social matters through a "preferential option" for the poor and disadvantaged (FC§§44,47).

It is appropriate that this challenge to live as Christians is laid before us at the same time that large state agencies have taken over the provision of these needs. Christian families cannot replace these welfare structures but they can provide real, loving care for the oppressed and afflicted while working to change the structures of oppression and affliction. Rosemary Haughton sums up the importance of families:

> In this time of upheaval when so many innocent people are being hurt, there is an almost prophetic quality about that passage from the Council's document which firmly, almost ruthlessly, sets the Christian family at the heart of the church's mission of compassion for the world which God loves so much.
>
> That, then, is the vocation of the family in the Church—to discover its identity, to fulfill its needs, to grow in unity and loyalty by responding—each in its own way—to the Christian vocation of loving service. In each age, the church has called on special kinds of people to carry out its work. There is always a need for the religious congregation and other dedicated single people who can devote their lives to work beyond the scope and skill of an ordinary family. But it does seem that the church has a need at this particular historical moment for what a family can best provide: the sense of intimacy, the personal touch, a human environment of ordinary warmth and friendliness and lovingness.
>
> Very many people have pointed to the impersonality of the big cities, the big organizations, and to the loneliness and despair of those who feel rejected and depersonalized in their misery. Families, just because they have a continuous, ordinary, everyday life of their own and don't exist *just* to provide help, can give the sense of belonging, a feeling of positive, future-facing life.[18]

It is possible to categorize the role of the family in a variety of ways. For example, the Vatican Synod Secretariat distinguishes the role of the family according to its association with the threefold mission of the people of God—the prophetic, sanctifying or priestly, and social or kingly mission.[19] However, for pragmatic reasons we will focus on the family's *inward* role toward its own members and its *outward* role directed toward other persons and society as a whole.

In referring to the *inward* role of the family, Pope John Paul II wrote:

> The relationships between the members of the family community are inspired and guided by the law of "free giving." By respecting and fostering personal dignity in each and every one as the only basis for value, this free giving takes the form of heartfelt acceptance, encounter and dialogue, disinterested availability, generous service and deep solidarity.

Thus the fostering of authentic and mature communion between persons within the family is the first and irreplaceable school of social life, an example and stimulus for the broader community of relationships marked by respect, justice, dialogue and love.

The family is thus, as the synod fathers recalled, the place of origin and the most effective means for humanizing and personalizing society: It makes an original contribution in depth in building up the world, by making possible a life that is, properly speaking, human, in particular by guarding and transmitting virtues and "values"(FC§43).

Being a parent is difficult. Being a parent in a Christian family is even more so. Society awards prizes, degrees, and income to educators, physicians, and priests; not to parents. What parents get, sometimes, is "Mom, Dad, I love you," or "I don't know how you ever did it." The pain, sorrow, and work that goes into raising a family and is rewarded with "I love you" is the heart of Christian stewardship. Compassion and sharing are the products of the process. We teach our children through precept and example. They in turn teach us to be more tolerant and compassionate. The best way to capture this process is through autobiographical notes.

"The year was 1963. Chuck was in his last year of graduate school. Mary Ellen was at home with six children—newborn, one-, three-, four-, six-, and seven-years-old. From November 1 to March 1, at least one of the children was sick every day. Needless to say we were all exhausted. Finally the doctor put the whole family on antibiotics. A month later Mary Ellen, still not recovered, went back to the doctor who said "you have pneumonia, go home to bed." Six small children, husband in school (and teaching), and mother goes to bed. A neighbor with eight children of her own came over and cooked, cleaned, and changed diapers, waited on Mary Ellen, and watched our children except when Chuck was home. A week later when Mary Ellen was well she asked our neighbor, "What can we ever do to repay you?" Her answer was "There is no way you can repay me, do it for someone else sometime."

"The year was 1968. A week earlier we had moved to a new house and friends called to say their house had burned and could they stay with us. They stayed a month. All told we were nineteen people. No one complained about doubling up in single beds, sleeping on the floor, or having no privacy."

"The year was 1970. Our niece was spending the summer with us. We got a call from the parish asking if we would take a fifteen-year-old girl who was having problems at home. Our children immediately made her feel a part of the family, sharing and fighting with her as a sister."

"The year was 1972. Neighbors down the street recently had been convicted of embezzling $90,000.[20] They failed to show up for sentencing and were arrested at a street corner while delivering papers. The mother said, 'Children, go to the Wilber's.' Seven children, ages two to thirteen, arrived at our door saying, 'Mom says stay here.' Later that day the mother called from jail asking us to take care of her children. If we didn't, they would be sent to a notorious children's center where beatings and molestations were an everyday occurance. A day later two police officers and two people from the welfare department came to the house. They said, 'we have come to take the children.' 'You are not taking them anywhere' Mary Ellen replied. 'You are willing to take care of them?' they said. We replied yes. 'Fine, thank you, good-bye,' they said.

"We were in a wonderful CFM (Christian Family Movement, see Appendix A) group at that time. We got together and agreed to take the children until the parents were out of jail. One family took two of the children, four other families took one each, and we kept one. Almost two years later the children returned to their parents."

"The year was 1977. One of our daughters had a friend who was the victim of divorced parents that were remarried. She was not welcome at either home. Our daughter brought her home for the weekend and she stayed four months."

"The year was 1979. One of our daughters was working with a Glenmary project in South Carolina. She helped to organize community support for unionization of the local J.P. Stevens textile mill, particpated in anti-Klan activity, and generally worked in community organizing. At this writing she is in New Orleans living and organizing with the poorest of the poor."

One of the primary functions of the family then is to educate its members by precept and example to see their duties and responsibilities as Christians. As the Second Vatican Council stated: "In the family, parents have the task of training their children from childhood to recognize God's love for all men. Especially by example they should teach them little by little to show concern for the material and spiritual needs of their neighbor. The whole of family life, then, would become a sort of apprenticeship for the apostolate."[21]

This process of formation is not a one-way street. Parents learn from their children and from the very process of family life. What do they learn? According to Eugene S. Geissler, "First of all, forgiveness." Children do not necessarily accept the beliefs of their parents. "Parents can't dismiss what has happened by blaming it entirely on others. Parents find that they made mistakes." Thus they need to forgive and to be forgiven. Second, "Compassion [which] signifies a special kind of growth and learning that reaches beyond one's own family. It is part of the necessary exchange to make humanity whole. I see only two ways to compassion. The natural way is through family life, through the vulnerability of loving, through the kind of commitment of loved ones that ends in suffering with others their miseries and griefs...In our confused and convoluted, twisted and fragmented world, we are confronted daily with those who are in need of our compassion. It is necessary only to be aware and capable of compassion."[22]

This is not intended to be a complete catalog of ways to educate children for Christian stewardship. Many other things can and should be done.

The inward focus on education naturally leads to an outward role for the family. Regarding the family's outward role, Pope John Paul II wrote in *Familiaris Consortio*:

> The family has vital and organic links with society since it is its foundation and nourishes it continually through its role of service to life: It is from the family that citizens come to birth and it is within the family that they find the first school of the social virtues that are the animating principle of the existence and development of society itself.
>
> Thus, far from being closed in on itself, the family is by nature and vocation open to other families and to society and undertakes its social role (FC§42).

This outward focus takes several forms. First, teaching children by example requires that the family reach outside of itself. Second, when and if the children become filled with an understanding of stewardship, they will take on as part of their life's work the alleviation of suffering.

It should be clear that the family must be seen as more than an end in itself. It must also be seen as a path leading into the larger world of society. As Christians we are called to go out from the family as individuals and to join in united effort with others.

Some new structures are necessary to channel this effort. Unfortunately, little thought has been given to the family as a mediating institution. One idea might be to revitalize the Christian Family Movement by incorporating some aspects of the *Comunidades de Base*. Appendix A sketches the nature of CFM and Appendix B that of the *Comunidades de Base,* or Basic Christian Communities. Individual families need help to fulfull their role as training grounds for the Christian apostolate. Parishes and groups of families must function as a network of mediating institutions. If this help is not forthcoming, family life will turn inward to escape the helplessness generated by the mega-institutions.

To conclude, our argument is that the growth of mega-institutions, both corporate and governmental, has undermined society's mediating institutions. It is the mediating institutions which always have given meaning to people's lives and through which, in turn, they have impressed their values on society. We must find ways to revitalize the mediating institutions, particularly the family, if we are to successfully cope with the problems facing us now and in the future.

NOTES

1. We are indebted to the work of Peter Berger for the following material. See his "In Praise of Particularity: The Concept of Mediating Structures," published in *The Review of Politics* (July, 1976) and in Walter Nicgorski and Ronald Weber (eds.), *An Almost Chosen People* (Notre Dame, Ind.: University of Notre Dame Press, 1976).

2. *Ibid.*, p. 133.

3. *Ibid.*, p. 134.

4. *Ibid.*

5. Adam Smith, *The Wealth of Nations* (Modern Library Edition: New York: Random House, 1937).

6. Adam Smith. *The Theory of Moral Sentiments* (London: Henry G. Bohn, 1861).

7. Fred Hirsch, *Social Limits to Growth* (Cambridge, Mass.: Harvard University Press, 1978), p. 141.

8. See R. H. Tawney, *Religion and the Rise of Capitalism* (New York: Harcourt, Brace and World, Inc., 1926) and Charles K. Wilber, "The New Economic History Re-examined: R. H. Tawney on the Origins of Capitalism," *The American Journal of Economics and Sociology*, Vol. 33, No. 3 (July, 1974), pp. 249-258.

9. Hirsch, pp. 128-29.

10. This casts new light on the recent attempts to construct theories of justice that are acceptable to all. See John Rawls, *A Theory of Justice* (Cambridge, Mass.: Harvard University Press, 1971) and the literature spawned by that work. The whole endeavor can be seen as an attempt to create a substitute moral law based on rationality rather than religion.

11. Berger, *Ibid.*

12. See particularly *Rerum Novarum, Quadragesimo Anno, Mater et Magistra, Pacem in Terris, Gaudium et Spec.*

13. Berger, p. 138.

14. See Proceedings of the Latin American Bishops Conference, Puebla, Mexico (Notre Dame, Ind.: CCUM, 1979).

15. "Toward the Synod of 1980: The Role of the Christian Family in Modern Society: Preliminary Paper of the Vatican Synod Secretariat," *Origins: NC Documentary Service*, Vol. 9, No. 8 (July 19, 1979), p. 115.

16. "Decree on the Apostolate of the Laity," *The Documents of Vatican II* (New York: Guild Press, 1966), p. 503.

17. "Toward the Synod of 1980," p. 127.

18. Rosemary Haughton, "Testimony on the Family," *Liberty and Justice for All: Atlanta Hearing* (National Conference of Catholic Bishops, Committee for the Bicentennial, August 9, 1975), p. 67.

19. "Toward the Synod of 1980," pp. 123 ff.

20. Ironically they were political right-wingers who stole the money from Liberty Lobby. But, Jesus said, "love your enemies."

21. "Decree on the Apostolate of the Laity," p. 518.

22. Eugene S. Geissler, "Our Children Our Greatest Teachers," in *Marriage Among Christians*, ed. James T. Burtchaell, C.S.C. (Notre Dame, Ind.: Ave Maria Press, 1977), pp. 58, 61-62.

APPENDIX A

An Overview of the Christian Family Movement

The Goals of the Christian Family Movement are to promote the Christian way of life in the family, in the families of the community, and in the institutions affecting the family by servicing, educating, and representing the family.

FOUNDERS OF CFM, 1949.

The development of people as described in the above statement occurs through the community achieved in the CFM group, by the study of Scripture, and use of the social inquiry method.

SOCIAL INQUIRY METHOD

CFM uses a method called the social inquiry method. The social inquiry method is a way of dealing with life through an *observe-judge-act* technique. We *observe* a situation from daily life, *judge* whether or not the situation needs a change, and agree to *act*. In acting both actor and situation change. CFM has used *observe*, *judge* and *act* because it does help couples to develop and to deal with problems.

Observations are the gift each member brings to the meeting. From observations the group can build discussion, judgment and action. Sometimes observations may be personal opinions or memories, but most often they are *outside information* which the couples gather before the meeting. Outside information enlarges the knowledge and perspective of the group; it is new learning. Without such information members are likely to *pool their ignorance* and learn nothing. Good leaders will promote good observations. Realizing the difficulties in collecting such information, they will *coach* their members in acquiring this skill. Most can do this best by telling how *they* do it and by actually doing it themselves.

Judgments are primarily personal matters, each member being influenced by his own point of view. Judgments, however, are also affected by group knowledge; therefore they are affected by *oberservations*. If possible, a group will obtain consensus. Realizing that agreement is not always possible, group members will be tolerant of unresolvable differences. As the group matures and as members feel more free to disagree, they will also feel more free to agree!

Information without evaluation and judgment is worthless. Similarly, judgment has less value until expressed and tested in *action*. Action is not required after every meeting, but action develops couples and matures the group.

Action may be individual or group-oriented. Sometimes individual actions will be personal and private. Often they can be decided upon by a group, although carried out by the individual or couple. Individual members or couples may differ greatly in what they believe can or should be done. Each should be heard. Realizing that members who feel they have had a chance to influence the group are more likely to accept the group's decision, good leaders will encourage thorough consideration of each possibility, particularly in the light of interests, talents, limitations and opportunities. They will not *railroad through* the action they want; neither will they permit louder and more agressive members always to determine the action.

Group actions are always arrived at by agreement among members. Because group actions are based on agreement and effected through cooperation, such actions contribute to *group spirit*, and because members recognize the educative effect of action—even when the action does not produce the effect they wanted—effective leaders will always reflect on actions with the group.

From: *Work, Money and Your Family* (CFM, 1976). Used with permission.

APPENDIX B

Human Betterment from Basic Christian Communities

Over the past twenty years Latin American Catholics have been experimenting with small groups of believers, much smaller and more localized than the typical parish, who pray, study their faith, and share a common Christian life together. They call these groups Basic Christian Communities.

... the Basic Christian Community does not replace the celebration of the Eucharist or the administration of the sacraments, but it does enable a group of two or three gathered in the name of Christ to find Christian faith quickened when they meet to worship in the intimacy of small neighborhood groups. Necessarily lay leadership and initiative are fostered.

With the bishop's approbation and encouragement, the lay leaders of these small basic communities direct the Liturgy of the Word and a discussion of the day's Epistle and Gospel readings, baptize, and, with special permission, officiate at weddings and distribute Communion.

... These communities are the basic unity of the Church where deeper prayer and shared values are lived, where personal and group objectives merge to question, discuss and act, and where ordinary people are given a sense of being the Church as a leaven in society and the world. Members of these small groups of Christians have a sense of responsibility for themselves as they celebrate the faith together. They form the Church as God's People rather than God's building.

JUSTICE AND PEACE, MAY 1977

From: *Understanding and Building Community* (CFM, 1977). Used with permission.

6

Rich Relationships
A Social Psychological Essay

Stanley L. Saxton, Ph.D.

THE UNIVERSITY OF DAYTON
DAYTON, OHIO

Michael A. Katovich, Ph.D.

TEXAS CHRISTIAN UNIVERSITY
FORT WORTH, TEXAS

At a Symbolic Interaction Symposium held at the University of Dayton during the spring of 1982, Dr. T. R. Young challenged the participants to discover the nature of rich and healthy human relationships. He also asked for the social processes and structural conditions necessary to promote and maintain rich relationships. The answer to Dr. Young's challenge would complement our understanding of Pope John Paul II's assertions that the family be considered a place of warm communion, an environment of community and love which nurtures our humanity:

> The family, which is founded and given life by love, is a community of persons: of husband and wife, of parents and children, of relatives. Its first task is to live with fidelity the reality of communion in a constant effort to develop an authentic community of persons (FC§18).

This essay is devoted to discussing the nature of rich relationships and to initially explore social structural conditions necessary for their development and maintenance. While an answer to the question "Do you know what rich human relationships are?" would be helpful, we find the question much like Saint Augustine's "Do you know the definition of time?" We did until asked. Others seem to have the same difficulty. As we look for exemplars of rich relationships in sociological literature, novels, films, and theater, we conclude that few are to be found. While our search continues, others who have worked with the above expressions have also had limited success (Hailey, 1968; Lennard and Bernstein, 1970; Watzlawic et al., 1968). We understand the nature of several kinds of relationships, but apparently not rich relationships.

This is not to imply that literature, film, and theater do not portray complex, deep, and strong relationships. Works like *King Lear, Death of a Salesman*, and *The Iceman Cometh*, for instance, provide the reader with a mosaic of themes concerning the human condition, but they also offer characters that become limited in a tragic sense and consequently impoverished. Several novels written in the early part of this century acquaint the reader with a richly textured group of characters. Dreiser's *The American Tragedy*, Fitzgerald's *The Great Gatsby*, and Sinclair's *The Jungle* offer descriptions of possibilities for rich relationships, but they also portray the miserable failure to consummate these possibilities or to create new possibilities that allow characters to escape from their tragic conditions. Edward Albee's *Who's Afraid of Virginia Woolfe?* and Rod Serling's *The Comedian* develop characters who commit themselves to a relationship but who cannot cope with the strain of their commitment. The reader of these works is introduced to a richly textured view of human life, but life portrayed in these novels is, in the end, barren of possibilities.

It seems that rich characterizations of relationships must be accompanied by a tragic vision. Yet, there is an abundance of "saccharine" portrayals of human relationships from *Love Story* to *Love Boat*. To many of us such offerings seem shallow and sterile. Perhaps intelligent portrayals of human relationships virtually assume a pessimistic point of view. To try to fully describe the various relationships we form may be perceived as compromising the reality of human relationships or as being ridiculously boring. Perhaps it is not the mission of art or social science to describe healthy human interaction. Fear of a Pollyannish treatment of the human condition may be so pervasive that only the tragic vision is considered legitimate.

Some writers imply that one can understand rich relationships through a contrast with vivid portrayals of impoverished conditions. This approach might be attributed to Victor Frankl, Bruno Bettelheim, and Alexander Solzhenitsyn who have given accounts of concentration camps. Frankl developed his theory of self-improvement on the basis of this kind of contrast. *One Day in the Life of Ivan Denisovich* is a classic example of the antithesis of interpersonal richness. Even contemporary political writers, such as John Dean (through his book *Blind Ambition*), seem to be warning us to change our ways and to do whatever is possible to act the opposite of what they describe. This approach does not appear to be strong, however. Richness is not to be equated with relationships that lack bitterness, competition, artfulness, depression, and delusion. It is not just the absence of pathology that makes relationships rich.

We think it is important to develop conceptual models of rich relationships in their own right. It is good to artistically portray, scientifically explain, and humanistically understand the difficulties of human relationships. But it is not simply the absence of difficulty that is ideal. That is not enough. The scientific study of deviance and the artistic portrayal of, or a deep understanding of, marital conflict and interpersonal violence is only half complete. Conceptions and models of interpersonal life that involve more than not violating someone's norms or hurting someone are needed to expand our sensibilities. In addition, we should provide conceptual maps for visualizing, recognizing, and developing rich relationships. We are convinced that one of the serious difficulties for ex-convicts, former mental patients, persons in troubled marriages, and others is that they have few experiences and ideas about what rich relationships are, to say nothing about how to create and maintain such relationships. If we do not have such visions, we may know what we do not want or do not like in a relationship, but do we know what will be satisfying in the long run?

It is common enough to portray rich relationships in modern romantic terms, or by highlighting feelings of warmth and security, or by stating, in normative fashion, that humans should love one another. Do we believe that being "rational" about these relationships in effect destroys their essence and mystery? Does scrutiny of rich relationships from a dispassionate standpoint contradict the emotional experience of having rich relationships? The popular strategy may be to avoid systematic analysis and thus maintain the ethos that these relationships are simple and pure. We must observe, however, that people do not just receive the gift of rich relationships; they construct them. How they construct them may appear mysterious, but it is unwise (if such relationships are valuable) to think simplistically about the processes of construction and to assume that to dismantle these processes is to strip them of their value. On the contrary, analyzing the nature of rich relationships may help us understand how they are developed and how they can be maintained. We seek this understanding with the hope that it will provide the foundation for more satisfying interpersonal relationships. We argue that rich relationships are, first of all, complex phenomena involving depth and breadth of feeling and information. Second, rich relationships are not simply dyadic, but are contextualized in a web of related interdependence which has implications for the social- and self-conceptions of each party to the relationship. As we develop each of these arguments, we will identify focal interpersonal process(es) and

describe social structural condition(s) supporting the enactment of processes necessary to experience a rich relationship.

DEPTH AND BREADTH OF BELIEF AND FEELING

The construction of rich relationships unfolds over time. It is an interpersonal behavioral process. Participants must develop both a depth
and breadth in their beliefs about the nature of each person and a history
of emotional experience involving a range of feelings and reactions. Rich
relationships are constructed by persons who have physical as well as social, emotional, and existential proximity with another person or other people. We may have rich relationships outside of our immediate environment,
but, with exceptions, these relationships were formed in the same environment. The importance of this observation is that interactional and interpersonal time spent with the other person across differing social situations
is necessary for the development of rich relationships. The more time spent
with another person, the more likely we will be able to observe each other
in the co-presence of other persons. We see how the other responds to us
and to others while in the company of superiors, subordinates, equals, and
friends of ours. We also see how others respond to the other person and to
us in relationship with the other person. How my friends respond to me is
known. How my friends respond to the other person and to me in relationship to the other person provides important information about "who"
the other person is and who I am in the co-presence of the other person.
There is no substitute for a mutual biography of interpersonal experience
across time and across social settings.

The contrast to this point is the simple stereotypical objectification of
an other. This often occurs when experience is confined to highly structured role relationships, such as, teacher/student, boss/worker. It can also
occur when our contacts are defined solely in terms of quantitative time.
We perform our functions for another according to external demands; for
example, physician/patient. Once these demands cease, the typical response is to abandon the relationship. When experiences are in highly
structured relationships and the demands of the clock become monoto-
nous, owing to the impossibility of fleeing, then the relationship becomes
impoverished. This is the basis of concentration camp accounts. Ivan Denisovich knew other prisoners only as prisoners and was a captive audience
with them, minute after minute, hour after hour. He knew these prisoners
within the basic environment of securng food and avoiding detention. These
prisoners were with each other for a considerable length of time, but they
did not go beyond the most expressionless of acts with each other. They

were quantitatively rich but qualitatively filled with the most redundant of experiences. Interpersonal experiences were shallow and relationships were impoverished.

In contrast, consider the intense attentiveness of new or rekindled sexual attraction. In this case, persons actively relate with one another. They provide each other with virtually a singular source of excitation as they construct an encounter of mutuality. Mutuality is sensual. It need not be, but often is, constructed between two persons who inform each other that they will provide and attend to each other as one, if not the exclusive source, of stimulus and emotion. In a mutuality experience we inform each other that each is the center of the other's attention. We demonstrate this centeredness by using the other's interests and behavior as the central source of our own behavior and interests. This exclusive reciprocal attentiveness and availability blurs the self/other distinction in its more intense moments, and therefore offers a blinded experience unique to that relationship at that point in time. It is novel not only to those participants but also to those participants at that point in their mutual history. Their individual and collective pasts are draw upon to provide the content of their mutuality. Their experience of mutuality will in turn become a part of their collective history to be drawn upon to construct a mutuality experience in the future.

SUPPORTIVE SOCIAL STRUCTURAL CONDITIONS

Demands and expectations external to the persons in the relationship can diminish the probability of developing or nurturing a rich relationship. If the parties are consumed by their occupations, parenting, and/or civic responsibilities, they will have little opportunity for qualitative interactional time. Persons require a certain amount of insulation from external demands so that they can have mutual experiences, and therefore construct interests, expectations, and understandings germane to their relationship and only to their relationship. Such understandings are built around the emerging information learned from each other through time. For this reason their interests are necessarily unique to their relationship as it develops through time. If participants are obliged to organize their interaction in response to external demands, they tell one another about their external interests, they do not talk about their own relationship. Their relationship then becomes stilted and shallow, and in the extreme, it becomes a vehicle for fulfilling external role obligations and interests, but it does not serve the obligations and interests of their own relationship. Women who learn to believe and feel that their principal, if not only, function in life is to serve the career interests of their husbands are poignant examples. A spouse serving their husband or wife is enriching even if the service and attention is not equally reciprocated. A spouse serving the career interests of a husband or wife, however, is impoverishing. The effort and emotion is swept outside the relationship, thus it is not a resource for the relationship.

Interaction becomes rich when participants mutually allow a multiplicity of topics to emerge during their encounter. If one party refuses to build off of the topics that interest the other and insists on a focus that only interests him, then interaction can become stilted and impoverished. Emergent interaction mutuality involves sensitivity to the interests of another as opposed to the controlling interests of one or the other. Controlled interaction normally involves an instrumental or task-like character. It denies the emergent expression of mutual interests. We often observe controlled interaction in physician/patient relationships. The patient may attempt to engage the physician in topics apart from the physician's professional task, while the physician's "civil inattention" clearly indicates that his professional focus is of central importance, not the development of a relationship.

The prototype of insulated interaction is play. Playful interaction is constructed when external demands and literalness are temporally suspended—interactants are given "room to roam" without accounting for their acts. Play also implies equality. Domination, subordination, and such notions of hierarchy are absent when people play. Play, however, tends to be episodic. Play is carved out of "real life" and marked off as separate from reality. After a play episode, actors return to more serious matters. In this sense, play is like a "time out" from the enterprise of living. It has no other purpose than to provide relief for interactants who must eventually return to their responsibilities.

INTERDEPENDENCE: NEAR AND DISTANT FUTURES

Two features of interpersonal relationships contribute to interdependence: the joint construction of mutual futures and mutual accountability. Much of the utility of human relationships involves the projection of near and distant futures. We regularly inform one another of our plans for being in certain places in order to perform particular activities. Much of this activity is mundane—"See you about five, Honey"; "I won't be home until seven; my meeting will run late this afternoon." Needless to say, without prediction of near futures it is difficult, if not impossible, to coordinate interpersonal (group) life. Suspend for three days your predictions of near futures—see what happens. Now, to the extent that our relationships are based on role performance, the organization within which our behavior occurs organizes near future predictions for us. Time clocks, date books, and meeting schedules are obvious examples. These kinds of schedules are not the material of rich relationships. They are the requirements of impersonal organizations. It is behavior prescribed by and for organizational interests, not interpersonal interests. The near future agreements we construct with other persons that are extraorganizational is the material of identifying, reassuring, and reaffirming the nature of our relationships. What we agree to do with and for one another is a significant part of how we establish the unique identity of our relationship.

This point is more dramatically made when we construct long-term futures. Humans are existential beings, and the future is fundamentally problematic with the exception of biological limitations and death; that is, I will not run a three-minute mile, and I will die. To arrange for an activity with another person six months from now, to say nothing of ten years from now, indicates that in the meantime our intention connotes a commitment to that other person and, of course, they to us. Constructing those long-term futures notifies both parties of their mutual intention to attend to and be with one another, at least at that distant time and most likely during the interim. The relationship takes on continuity that extends beyond the everyday coordination of near futures and is unique to the relationship simply because it is the plans for the distant future not predicted for us by organizational interests but constructed by us for our mutual interests.

The construction of shared futures often involves the mutual construction of objectives; for example, we discuss and agree to invest our time in fixing the house next year and not to travel. Deciding on which objective is most agreeable to the participants is negotiable in rich relationships and is not unilaterally determined. The negotiation process involves differences in interests and the resolution of these differences through discussion of options and the search for possible areas of agreement. We may agree to one objective as we simultaneously consider the possibility of others. On the other hand, a hidden agenda by one party circumvents the process of negotiation. When one has a hidden agenda, that party informs the other that their interests are more important than the development of mutual interests and the construction of mutual futures.

A husband, for instance, may wish to use expendable funds to improve the house. He will not do this unless his wife agrees to this use of funds. The wife's agreement, however, is never made. She does not disagree that using expendable funds to improve the house is a good idea, but she does not provide support for this use. This leaves the husband in an untenable and nonnegotiable position. Alternatives are not provided and a decision is not made. The husband is in the uncomfortable position of having to continually broach the subject to his wife without receiving a reciprocal indication of interest. The implication here is that the wife has a hidden agenda which leaves the problem suspended in mid-air.

A hidden agenda is behaviorally expressed in the subtle unwillingness to directly discuss a future desired by the other. In this situation there is neither disagreement nor agreement, rather a strategy of avoiding the issue. If pressed, the other may agree or disagree with a projected future, but in doing so they make it painfully clear that the decision is not "their" decision but, instead, a compliance to the wishes of the other. An actual or perceived abundance of these kinds of reluctantly agreed-to futures can undermine a relationship. The satisfaction and exclusiveness of a relationship comes in part from a history of successfully constructed mutual futures. If they have not been genuinely mutual, then the foundation of understandings which results from a history of mutual futures is problematic. What is taken for granted in a relationship by virtue of having been worked through in the past and assumed to be understood in the present is not secure if it has only been agreed to under duress; that is, if a previous agreement was merely compliance. Whether past futures were constructed through genuine mutual agreement or through compliance in the context of hidden agenda is not the central issue. What is more important is how past agreements are later perceived to have occurred. If either party believes that past agreements were built around a mere pretext of the mutual construction of futures—that is, compliance—then the legitimacy of past understandings as brought forward to contextualize present discussion of futures may be questioned. Hidden agenda in the present construction of the future can call into question the legitimacy of understandings built during the history of the relationship.

INTERDEPENDENCE: ACCOUNTABILITY

Accountability is the process of asking another person for an explanation of untoward behavior. It assumes that a reasonable expectation for activity has been violated or unfulfilled. All relationships involve holding one another accountable for "broken promises," but an essential element in the process of accountability in ongoing relationships is who holds whom accountable, how accountability is expressed, and how accounts are provided. A major consideration is the symmetry of accountability by both members of the relationship.

One-sided or unilateral accountability occurs when one person in the relationship expresses expectation for the other's behavior and holds that person accountable for fulfilling those expectations. Mutual or bilateral accountability occurs when both parties express expectations for each other's behavior and hold each other accountable for conforming to those expectations. The unilateral accountability needs little comment except in respect to degree of asymmetry. Highly one-sided accountability is a tyrannical relationship wherein the one person controls the behavior of the other—a reasonably rare occurrence. One-sidedness of lesser degree is usually the case; nevertheless, it is a difficult situation for the subordinate person, particularly when asymmetry is capricious, or unpredictable, for the subordinate. When the superordinate party unexpectedly violates an expectation and refuses to be held accountable by not providing an account or by providing a rationale that is not consistent with mutual understandings, the subordinate is "put in their place" and thus experiences alienation from the relationship. If the superordinate draws upon a "power role" external to the relationship, the subordinate is notified that their interests are secondary to the external role requirements; that they and their relationship do not occupy the place of first importance.

The consequences of mutual accountability for a relationship are subtle in that they have implications for the very nature of how the persons in a relationship individually control themselves. Mutual accountability does not simply refer to holding one another accountable when an expectation is violated. The deeper meaning of mutual accountability is that each party understands that it is the right of the other to have expectations for their conduct, and to hold them accountable for expected conduct. Furthermore, it is the obligation of the person being held accountable to provide an accounting which is consistent with understandings within the relationship.

Mutual accountability signifies a deep relationship and each party's understanding that the relationship is of high priority for influencing their behavior. It indicates that each party has decided to give up the degree of freedom allowed those in a more independent relationship. It demonstrates one to the other that they are willing to subordinate themselves to the relationship by holding and being held accountable for conforming to mutually constructed near and distant futures. Mutual accountability is the ongoing public indicator of the importance of an interdependent relationship.

A history of successful mutual accountability in a relationship has significant implications for the self-conception of the participants. Being held accountable and offering a satisfactory account is not usually a rewarding experience. It involves being told that your behavior is not acceptable and being asked to explain the untoward behavior. Not all reasons for the behavior are acceptable, given the mutual understandings of the relationship.

If it is the right of the other to hold one accountable and if a "reasonable account" is not, or cannot be, provided in good faith, a threat to the relationship has occurred.

It is important to note that in an accountability episode a loss of face is experienced by both parties. An expectation of the person calling for an account has been violated and the person offering no account or an inappropriate account is guilty of breach of understanding. A willingness to lose face is public testimony to the reality and value of the relationship, however difficult or painful it may be for both participants. Being held accountable and holding another accountable is the evidence of the significance and reality of the relationship. A history of negotiating such episodes successfully informs both members that they have a mutual biography of self-sacrifice which sustains the relationship and maintains their self-conception in the context of their relationship.

The contextualized self-conception has the effect of obliging the parties to be careful about placing one another in the position of holding and being held accountable for untoward activity. In mutual accountability one does not have an external role to hide behind when holding another accountable. For this reason, in mutual accountability relationships, selves are exposed and are vulnerable. Selves are intertwined with, and dependent upon, the relationship; thus, they are mutually exposed through holding or being held accountable. For this reason, we are likely to observe a heightened sensitivity to avoiding untoward activity; that is, we exercise much more self-control vis-a-vis one another in relationships involving mutual accountability.

SUPPORTIVE CONDITIONS: WEBBED INTERPERSONAL RELATIONS

Two-person groups are notoriously brittle. In all our uniqueness, our shifting moods, attention, and interests, it goes without saying that a relationship that depends only upon another person is feeble. However tolerant, understanding, and loving we are as persons, we know how easily a relationship can be ruptured, perhaps destroyed, by a single indiscretion. One infidelity, an evening of angry words, a flash of temper, discovery of fundamental differences can do serious damage to, perhaps destroy, a relationship of years standing. Rarely do rich relationships stand upon the shifting quirks of individuals. Rather, they are embedded in ongoing mutually valuable relationships with many other people. It is the embedded nature of this web of interpersonal relationships which provides the interpersonally supportive foundation allowing for, perhaps obliging, the patience and discretion to be tolerant and understanding of each other. If the existence of a relationship is a condition for the maintenance of other important interpersonal relationships with family, friends, and children, then both parties have a stake in maintaining the relationship which goes beyond the temporary and unique characteristics of each person at any one point in time. In fact, as we have seen, the richness of a relationship is in large part built upon a history of negotiating and surviving temporary problems (however difficult in the short run). Having the time and finding it possible to come to a mutual understanding at juncture one is a legacy that demonstrates the possibility of mutual understanding at a future date. We know how rich and strong our relationships are through the understanding generated by past coping with "temporary" problems.

Being embedded in a web of relationships has another important function for mutual relationships. However interesting a person or two persons might be, they, as sole resources of information for the relationship, have limitations. They run the risk of becoming redundant, perhaps boring. When a relationship is a part of a wider set of mutual relationships, however, the sources of interesting information become geometrically more complex and resourceful. Not only does the couple have knowledge of what other parties are experiencing ("going through"), their other relationships can bring them interpersonal contacts beyond themselves and thus add stimulation and additional sources of topics and issues for discussion.

The stability of place of residence and social status required to sustain a mutually important web of relations is difficult to maintain in a society that fosters geographic and vertical mobility. While it is possible to sustain relationships through writing and telephone, there is no substitute for periodic face-to-face interaction. Face-to-face interaction provides the mutual and simultaneous communication with another or others that is necessary for joint experiences. When just one party of the relationship pairs off with another or others, this creates exclusive, not inclusive, experiences. And it is the mutual experiences of important other(s) which is important for rich relationships. If, for example, a future wife only goes to see her parents by herself while her fiancé continues to visit his parents alone, they do not mutually experience each other's parents. In consequence, he must experience her parents through her description and vice versa. They do not directly experience a relationship with each other's parents. Her parents' influence on him and his parents' influence on her is minimal. The fabric of this "web" is loosely strung for it is the mutual influence of another relationship that is important to support their relationship.

Loosely strung webs of relationships separate from the couple's primary relationship are more influential than no web at all. Webs can also become, however, too entangling and thus create external demands which reduce the richness of the relationship. Trying to maintain too many relationships can be self-defeating. As with external organizational demands, an entangling web of relationships can threaten the interactional time necessary to maintain rich relationships. A couple that lives in the same neighborhood with a half dozen brothers and sisters may find that that supportive community so occupies their time and energy that they find it difficult to insulate themselves from familial concerns. In effect, they find themselves "spread too thin" in maintaining these familial relationships. We are not sure what an optimum number of mutually important webs of relationships might be—it is an empirical question yet to be investigated.

If the richness of a two-person relationship is exclusive only to those persons, resources to sustain the relationship are limited. We have argued that rich relationships involve mutual depth and breadth of information and feeling, mutual construction of near and distant futures, mutual accountability. The members of a two-person relationship are interpersonally unequal if one person has substantially fewer resources than the other; for example, knowledge about topics relevant to the conditions of the relationship; capacity to experience and express a range of emotions; ability to define, analyze, and articulate solutions to problems pertaining to the relationship; and skills to contribute goods and services necessary to sustain the material well-being of the relationship. This inequality will likely result in expressions of a superordinate-subordinate form of relating to one another, and this will significantly reduce the mutuality of constructing futures and accountability. When a two-person relationship is embedded in a mutually supportive web of relationships, the stronger of the two persons can influence those other relationships and the weaker can draw additional resources from those relationships to maintain his/her position of equity in the primary relationship.

Finally, and equally important, when relationships unfold within a context of webbed relationships, each person can "escape" the primary relationship. To be the exclusive source of sustenance for a relationship is at times a difficult and tedious task. In the case of married couples, for each to be able to give to, and draw from, other relationships provides a haven from the periodic intensity of their spousal obligations. When spouses take "time out" with others who have a relationship important to both spouses, the legitimacy and exclusiveness of their relationship is not questioned. They are interacting within and contributing to the community from which both spouses benefit.

Conclusions

Pope John Paul II states that the family should be an "intimate community of life and love." The family has the mission to become more and more what it is. He goes on to say, "conjugal communion constitutes the foundation on which is built the broader communion of the family." We agree with this assessment. We also believe that wisdom concerning conjugal love and the family includes the contribution that social analysis can bring to our understanding of interpersonal relationships. The ability to be empathetic and to love is unique to humans and an invaluable capacity which must be nurtured in the context of rich interpersonal relationships. Without that supportive environment, this ability has a tendency to erode. We must be mindful of the fact that we humans have the capacity for indifference, objectification, and calculating approaches to our fellow human beings. We can be not only loving and generous but also tyrannical and selfish.

In our opinion, we are obliged to understand both faces of interpersonal relationships so that we can encourage empathy and generosity. We dare not assume empathy or love nor simply prescribe it. We must, instead, seek to understand how it is possible in the everyday lives of people. Families must have, and be encouraged to use, their time to interact, to develop, and to sustain complex beliefs and feelings about one another. We must recognize that the demands of impersonal organizations, whether they be a church, workplace, school, or civic group, can intrude upon the family's ability to construct their near and distant futures. Furthermore, we must support mutual accountability, realizing that persons are tempted to use personal capacities or external demands to justify either not making spousal or family commitments or to explain away their broken promises to family members on the basis of external demands.

If we believe the family is the first and vital cell of society from which new human life emanates and is served, the communion of persons is first and most fully experienced within primary relationships. To sustain families as examples of community respect, justice, dialogue, and love, we must act to hold external organizations accountable for intruding upon the family's capacity to be what it should be. Finally, we must not insulate the family from a web of mutually supportive community relationships. We must raise consciousness to the effects rapid geographic and social mobility may have on the richness of spousal and family relationships. We must encourage family members to have, first, loyalty to themselves and to those who nourish their relationships so that a reciprocal growth of strength and depth is possible.

REFERENCES

Hailey, Jay. 1968. "An Interactional Explanation of Hypnosis." In D. D. Jackson (ed.), *Therapy Communication and Change*. Palo Alto, California: Science and Behavior Books.

Lennard, H. L. and A. Bernstein. 1970. *Patterns in Human Interaction*. San Francisco, California: Jossey-Bass.

Pope John Paul II. 1981. "The Apostolic Exhortation on the Family." *Origins* XI, 28 and 29 (December 24):443. Washington, D.C.

Watzlawic, Paul, Janet H. Beavin and Don D. Jackson. 1968. *Pragmatics of Human Communication*. New York: W. W. Norton.

PART THREE

Female and Male Role Changes

Introduction

The position of *Familiaris Consortio* on the roles of men and women at work and in the home must be viewed in the context of several recent social and economic changes. The joint effects of inflation and recession over the past ten years have reduced the standard of living of many families and have increased the incidence of economic uncertainty. The Majka paper documents the severe and uneven effects of inflation and recession on families. Those most affected include women, minorities, and the elderly.

A second major social change in recent years is increased employment among married women. Dana Hiller discusses several factors contributing to this increase including the demand for labor, decreases in fertility and mortality rates, and increased levels of education among women. Voydanoff cites predictions that women's continuous employment over the life course will increase significantly over the next two decades.

A third critical change involves the expectations and behavior among men and women in the areas of work and family. Hiller sees this change as the extension of liberal democracy to women. However, the increased life choices of women conflict with expectations that women will continue to perform traditional homemaking and child-rearing roles. This dilemma is resulting in major changes in the views of how work and family responsibilities should be divided between men and women and in the actual distribution of responsibilities. In addition, work organizations are being asked to develop policies to accommodate these changes.

The exhortation *Familiaris Consortio* addresses three major issues that are relevant to these economic and social changes. The first refers to the need for equality between men and women (FC§23). Women should have equal access to public roles and offices. Sex discrimination should be eliminated (FC§24).

Secondly, the papal exhortation, at the same time it advocates equal dignity and public access for women, argues for recognizing the irreplaceable value of women's work in the home. In addition, society should provide conditions favoring women's home role and eliminate the economic necessity for women's outside employment (FC§23).

The third major issue raised in the document is the role of men as husbands and fathers. Husbands should consider marriage as a special personal friendship and reciprocate their wives' attentions. Fathers need to increase their role as the educators of children and their presence in the family without this presence being oppressive (FC§25).

The document and the papers by Majka, Hiller, and Voydanoff reveal the breadth and complexity of the issues involved in the changing roles of men and women. The document advocates the harmonious combination of work and family roles for men and women without explicitly recognizing the need for changes in employment policy to facilitate this goal. The document also provides a framework through which women and men can achieve equal dignity. However, it tries to do this in the context of different vocations for men and women. The Hiller and Voydanoff papers suggest that similar vocations may contribute to the achievement of equal dignity between men and women, greater value for homemaking and child rearing, and increased participation by men in family activities.

7

The Impact of Recent Economic Change on Families and the Status of Women

Linda C. Majka, Ph.D.

THE UNIVERSITY OF DAYTON
DAYTON, OHIO

For some time now social scientists have recognized that economic conditions have an impact on the quality and structure of family life. The availability of material resources affects the ability of families to offer love and protection. Changes in income and status affect family stability and happiness. Insecurity of economic means and inability to make ends meet affect family relationships.

The importance of financial security to the family deserved a more prominent place in the papal exhortation on the family. The document would have made a more powerful statement if it had made a central issue of the connection between material security and social relationships, the rights of families to a decent standard of living, and the rights of heads of households to organize to secure political and economic necessities. Many of the arguments with respect to the dignity of the worker presented in the encyclical on labor could have been addressed also to the struggle for the security of families. Furthermore, family issues must not be considered apart from women's efforts worldwide to gain equal dignity, or from the larger social context of the interests of minorities and the poor throughout the world.

One of the most striking changes recently affecting the American family has been the level of economic stress placed upon the household. Within the last fifteen years, our society has experienced three major recessions. The first occurred in 1969-70; the second in 1974-75; and the third began in 1980. Each of these recessions was related in some way both to the problems generated by inflation and to policies that were meant to solve those problems. In this paper I will argue that the combination of recession and inflation during these years has resulted in a sharp decline in the American standard of living. This has had a negative impact on the quality of family life. Furthermore, the unfavorable effects of economic decline place the greatest burden on those least able to bear the cost. I intend to give special attention to the impact upon women, but the uneven distribution of costs of these recessions also weighs heavily upon the poor, the elderly, and minorities. While we can generalize about the observed effects of recessions on the family, it is well to keep in mind that the full social consequences of economic stress will take years to be fully realized.

The White House Conference on the Family in 1980 recognized three major forms of economic pressures on households: inflation, unemployment, and poverty.[1] These have been identified as contributing to family violence, juvenile delinquency and runaways, alcohol and drug abuse, and separation and divorce. Joblessness and inadequate incomes undermine family stability.[2] While dual-career families have a buffer against privations of inflation, they, like traditional families, have experienced a drop in real incomes.[3] Social scientists have known for some time that social pathology is tied to income and employment status. Mortality rates increase along with increases in the unemployment rate. The rise in mortality is most dramatic for infants and the elderly, who are more susceptible to illness. The suicide rate is so sensitive to shifts in employment that it can be virtually used as an economic indicator.[4]

RECESSIONS AND FAMILY SECURITY

The severe inflation of the 1970s caused major dislocations in the economy and particular hardship on those at the bottom of the income scale. During the seventies consumer prices essentially doubled, by increasing at an annual rate of over 7 percent. In comparison, during the sixties consumer prices rose only 2.3 percent annually, and in the fifties by 2.0 percent.[5] The principal reason inflation is so damaging is that it is directly related to the basic means of life: food, fuel, medical care, and housing. The poor and near-poor are disproportionately affected because, according to one study, the bottom 20 percent of the population spends 90 percent of their income on the basics. For the bottom 10 percent the cost of subsistence is more than they earn.[6]

Rising energy costs, along with mortgage interest rates, have accounted for as much as three-quarters of the acceleration in inflation in recent years.[7] For low-income families the percentage of income that is spent on energy is four times more than it is for the rest of the population,[8] even though they consume less total energy than more prosperous households. This is so in spite of the fact that they are located in housing that is less energy efficient and penalizes their efforts at conservation.[9]

While the cost of living has risen over 100 percent since 1969, many states have cut the real level of welfare payments simply by refusing to raise them according to the cost of living. The same dollar amount in a welfare check buys less than half of what could have been purchased by a family receiving it in 1967. States have also sought to eliminate families from the welfare rolls by failing to increase the dollar amount of cutoffs used to determine eligibility.[10] In 1980 the average monthly payment of AFDC (Aid to Families with Dependent Children) was under $300 for a family of three. Even the combination of food stamps and AFDC does not bring a family up to the official poverty level.

Inflation in the costs of necessities has a particularly severe impact on the elderly. Price rises for essentials like energy and medical care have risen faster than general price levels. The elderly on fixed incomes have no way to get additional money in order to compensate for this inflation. Each day the elderly population increases by a net of a thousand persons. Many of these are forced into a life style that is below the American standard of living because of the rising costs of the essentials.[11]

The chance of becoming unemployed during a recession depends on race, sex, and the family's normal or average income. Within each income class, black male heads-of-families experience more unemployment during recessions than white males. Among white male heads-of-families, the poor have a probability of experiencing unemployment that is twice as great as in the middle class.[12] With rises in unemployment during recessions, there are losses in family income that are only partially compensated for by relief in taxes and unemployment insurance and other transfers. Given the unequal distribution of these losses, the people forced by public policy to fight the war against inflation are those who can least afford the costs.[13]

Even workers who manage to retain their jobs during recessions suffer the fear of job loss that accompanies economic reversals. Also, they can expect to experience shorter hours and lower earnings.[14] Dual-earner families, along with traditional ones, have recently found their real earnings falling after inflation was taken into account.[15] A second income became a necessity for many families during the seventies. Within the middle class there are recession-induced cutbacks in food, energy use, and other essentials. Many find they are not able to afford housing that is better suited to the needs of their families, or college educations for their children.[16]

RECESSIONS AND OPPORTUNITY

Even in the best of times, women's rights to economic security and equal dignity are problematic in American society. The three recessions have seriously undermined the means of survival for millions of women in the United States. These economic contractions have eroded gains in the employment of women, created severe hardships for their families, and contributed to a feminization of poverty. The response of public policy during the current recession is compounding the losses women are experiencing.

The stereotyping of women workers as employable only within a narrow range of female occupations limited the jobs available to women newly entering the labor market in the seventies and early eighties. Two-thirds of the influx of female workers was absorbed into the service-producing sector that traditionally employs women: the services industry, finance, insurance, real estate, and retail trade.[17] Not incidentally, these are occupations that are characterized by low pay: average weekly earnings in the service sector are about two-thirds of earnings in the goods sector. Eighty percent of all employed women work in the service sector.

Women generally experience higher jobless rates than do men in major occupational groups within each sector. In job areas that only recently relaxed the barriers against female workers, women are not able to accumulate much seniority. Thus, the recessions subject them more to layoffs. For example, during the 1973-75 decline, women in manufacturing were affected by cutbacks more severely than men.[18] While service employment where women are concentrated tends to have lower jobless rates than the goods sector where men are concentrated, the current recession is also causing job curtailments in the more stable service sector. Even among women who succeed in remaining employed, there are losses in income due to recession-induced cutbacks in hours and earnings.

Unemployment statistics relating to women do not entirely explain the overall impact of economic decline, because a major effect of recessions on women workers is discouragement from job-seeking.[19] Economic slack causes women who want to be employed to drop out of the labor market because of the depressing lack of opportunity. Women and minorities are experiencing a disproportionate share of the increase in "discouraged" workers during the current recession. Women accounted for 63 percent of all discouraged workers at the end of 1982, although they composed only 43 percent of the working-age population. Blacks, who accounted for 32 percent of the discouraged, constituted 13 percent of the working-age group.

A report made recently by the U.S. Civil Rights Commission[20] documents that women experienced disproportionate rates of underemployment throughout the seventies and early eighties. They work part time when they prefer, but are unable to find full-time work. Their jobs tend to be marginal, intermittent, or low-skill types of employment. Women are more likely than men to receive poverty-level pay or pay that does not match their education, training, and experience. These disadvantages apply across age and educational categories.

Discrimination continues to cause a lag in women's earnings relative to men's. One survey on the status of women who are heads of households was reported to the 1980 White House Conference on Families. The results of the survey revealed that these women were paid less than men with comparable education and training; and that over half of these families would have risen above poverty level if the women had been paid a wage equal to men of similar training and experience.[21]

Women bear an unequal share of the losses due to long-term unemployment. Long-term unemployment is a major source of stress because it leads to economic hardships and poverty. While black men are more likely to experience long-term unemployment than white men, all women have higher rates than men. Women maintaining households are three times more likely to suffer from long-term unemployment than do men.[22]

Children are the indirect victims of the dual effects of economic decline and women's unequal status. Many of their mothers entered the labor force in the seventies and early eighties during deteriorating labor conditions when a second income became a necessity for many families. According to the U.S. Department of Labor, by March 1981, 54 percent of all children under 18—31.8 million children—had mothers who were looking for work or were employed.[23]

Millions of children are now partially or wholly dependent upon their mothers' earnings. In March 1981, one out of four children, or 14.8 million, lived in a family where the father was unemployed, out of the labor force, or absent. These circumstances affected two out of ten white children, and five out of ten black children. When the mother was in the labor force, the median income in 1980 of families with children was increased by $6500 when the father was unemployed, by $7100 when the father was out of the labor force, and by $5500 when the father was absent.[24]

Women's labor force experience is not the only area of economic status adversely affected by the recessions. Their economic status in general is undergoing a reversal. The recession years witnessed the extension of a "feminization of poverty." The numbers of families maintained by women is increasing: since 1970 the proportion of families headed by women rose from 11 percent to 18 percent. At the same time, the probability that women or women household heads (especially minorities) will live in poverty is becoming greater than for males or male household heads (especially whites). Poverty affects one out of nineteen husband-wife families, one out of nine families maintained by men, and one out of three families maintained by women. The composition of the class in poverty is thus shifting to one composed of more women and minorities than was the case before. Among the elderly poor, 81 percent are women. Half of the elderly women lacked the means to live in modest comfort during the past decade.[25]

In the current recession, the decline in opportunities for women is all the more serious because it is accompanied by the erosion of the institutional defenses against discrimination and poverty. Cutbacks in funding for the enforcement of civil rights statutes and regulations, and the disinterest of the Reagan administration in action favorable to women's employment signals the possibility for their greater exploitation. At the same time, the availability of child care declines as federal support for these services is withdrawn. Training programs that could help women escape the cycle of poverty are reduced. Welfare benefits are cut. Support for legal sevices for the poor, including those that protect the legal status of dissolutions, child custody determinations, and other elements of family law affecting them, is also cut.

The result of cutbacks in federal support for protections for women's employment and family support services is a substantial decline in the institutional means for women to maintain and defend their well being. Even as women's employment prospects become more difficult to realize, other means of subsistence and support services are disappearing.

WOMEN AND SOCIAL CHANGE

Collective efforts were necessary to achieve whatever improvements were made in the status of women in the past. Organizing by urban poor minority and white women led to the expansion of welfare and other programs of social assistance to families. Protest by the urban poor led to a larger variety of assistance in child care, low-cost housing, medical care, food, and energy. Feminist agitation led to commitments on the part of government at all levels to affirmative action and anti-discrimination laws and regulations. Identification with elements of feminist agendas and mobilization of collective resources by women throughout the society led to important changes in expectations for women. Greater choice in life options and opportunities in politics and the economy were a result of women's struggles.

Recessions, however, pose substantial dilemmas for groups who wish to organize for change in public policy. Difficulties arise because recessions do not affect all segments of the population in the same way. It is certainly more difficult for women to promote solidarity and work toward collective goals when economic conditions have a differential impact upon them depending upon their social class membership. The poor and near-poor are the most harshly affected because, to begin with, their incomes are barely enough for necessities. Many in the middle class are affected by recessions not in terms of present living standards but only with respect to their plans for the future. At still higher income levels, people may actually be experiencing an improvement in their circumstances as inflation moderates (although at the cost of unemployment for many others).

The problem of unemployment may be perceived primarily as a class issue rather than one of gender. The husband's unemployment has a worse impact on the economic security of a husband-wife household than the wife's. For example, in 1980 the median income of families in which only the husband was unemployed was 19 percent below the median for families in which a family member not the husband was jobless. Although the greater financial impact of the husband's unemployment is due to the underpayment of women's work, many people might regard the effect of men's unemployment as more serious. In addition, when the current recession deepened in 1982, men became jobless at a more rapid rate than women until their jobless rate equaled and surpassed women's: men's losses reached 11.1 percent, compared to women's 10.1 percent in the last quarter of 1982. Although women ordinarily have higher unemployment rates than men, the current recession caused sharp cutbacks in blue-collar occupations in the goods sector, where men are traditionally concentrated. Because women are underrepresented in these occupations, their jobless rate did not rise as rapidly. If women are perceived as intermittent and surplus workers, then the level of men's unemployment, although only one percent higher, might be considered a greater hardship. Examples like these suggest that many women and men will be more likely to understand the problem of unemployment primarily in terms of class rather than gender status.

The fact that minorities experience economic decline differently from whites creates the possibility that policy issues will be defined on the basis of race rather than of gender. Unemployment affects blacks more quickly and more severely than whites. Their recovery from previous recessions is weaker. Their unemployment level begins to rise earlier when a recession sets in. During the current recessions, blacks had record jobless rates from the beginning. During the last three months of 1982, their unemployment was over 20 percent. Unemployment of Hispanics was up to 15.2 percent. In the same quarter, white workers averaged 9.3 percent. The persistence of racial discrimination, despite the efforts to dislodge its institutional roots, influences minority women to define their struggle as primarily one of race.

The feminist movement can have an important part to play in protest against the effects of public policy during a recession. Women have long been witness to the fact that the economy does not automatically create equal opportunity, even in relatively prosperous years. Instead, women's options are circumscribed to poverty-level subsistence, low paid work, or persistent discrimination in private and public employment. At the same time, societal expectations continue to subject women to a disproportionate responsibility for domestic labor and child care. What improvements have been achieved in the status of women were won by insurgency; nothing was conceded to women in the public or private economy in advance of their protest struggles.

There is no logical reason why the defense of the human right to subsistence is incompatible with the struggle for equal dignity. Concretely, however, to combine both concerns suggests a change in feminist strategy. Women's organizations must develop agendas that challenge the feminization of poverty. The constituency of feminism cannot be widened without taking account of the perspective of poor, working-class, and nonwhite women. Political strategies will need to be more complex to balance the desire to advance the political careers of women candidates with the need to support candidates accountable to nonwhites and the poor. Strategies must be more sensitive to the need for social change relative to class and racial dimensions as well as gender. Enduring gains in the conditions of survival and well being are unlikely without advances that involve all three dimensions because their effects are thoroughly intertwined in the lives of women.

Conclusion

Practically speaking, this analysis suggests several implications for future change. We might well examine the costs of the war against inflation as it has been carried on to the present time. From much of the available information, the effects of the policy response to the problems of inflation have been to create uneven hardships. It is evident to growing numbers of people that the Reagan experiment has failed to maintain the material security we take as a necessary precondition to building our family lives and friendships.

The need for a shift in policy in response to the needs of families is clear. In the last months of the Carter administration, when it became evident that the country was headed for a new recession and public policy was not being established to counter or reverse it, there began to emerge a consensus among some of Carter's critics as to what should be done. The central priorities were to institute new economic policies directed toward the creation of full employment and controlling inflation in the prices of necessities. These policies were to be carried out with the awareness of the uneven impact of economic decline on segments of the population and geographical areas. These solutions would almost certainly require more economic planning than we have previously instituted.

To sum up these observations places me in the ambiguous position of a sociologist at a philosophical conference offering political-economic conclusions. As a society we cannot afford the social costs and waste in the form of personal suffering connected with undermining a major institution such as the family by the slow and painful process of economic deprivation. Solutions to the problems of family security are within reach of our current economic framework, but will not be achieved without a major political mobilization, in which women have a critical part to play.

NOTES

1. White House Conference on Families, *Families and Economic Well-Being* (Washington, D.C.; U.S. Government Printing Office, 1980), p. 11.

2. *Ibid.*, p.7.

3. Howard Hayghe, "Husbands and Wives as Earners: An Analysis of Family Data," *Monthly Labor Review*, 104, No. 2 (February, 1981), p. 50.

4. Dr. Harvey Brenner, *Hearings*, Part 37, Committee on Labor and Human Resources, U.S. Senate, 96th Congress, 2d Session (Washington, D.C.: U.S. Government Printing Office, July 24, 1980), p. 24.

5. "The Economy of 1981: A Bipartisan Look," *Proceedings* of a Congressional Economic Conference, December 10, 1980, Joint Economic Committee, 97th Congress, 1st Session (Washington, D.C.: U.S. Government Printing Office, April 20, 1981), p. xii.

6. "Impact of Inflation and Recession on Low Income Families," *Hearings*, Committee on the Budget, U.S. Senate, 96th Congress, 1st Session, Toledo, Ohio, August 21, 1979 (Washington, D.C.: U.S. Government Printing Office, 1980), p. 38.

7. "Impact of Energy Prices and Inflation on American Families," *Hearings*, Subcommittee on Energy, Joint Economic Committee, 96th Congress, 2d Session, July 8, 1980 (Washington, D.C.: U.S. Government Printing Office, 1981), p. 34.

8. *Ibid.*, p. 14.

9. *Ibid.*, p. 19.

10. *Ibid.*, p. 17.

11. *Hearings*, Committee on the Budget, pp. 9-11.

12. Isabel V. Sawhill, *Hearings*, Part 18, Joint Economic Committee, 97th Congress, 1st Session (Washington, D.C.: U.S. Government Printing Office, 1981), p. 248.

13. *Ibid.*

14. *Hearings*, Committee on Labor and Human Resources, p. 47.

15. Hayghe, p. 50.

16. *Hearings*, Committee on the Budget, pp. 1-6.

17. Howard Davis, "Employment Gains of Women by Industry, 1968-1978," *Monthly Labor Review*, 103, No. 6 (June, 1980), pp. 3-5.

18. *Ibid.*, p. 8.

19. Sawhill, p. 243.

20. U.S. Commission on Civil Rights, *Unemployment and Underemployment Among Blacks, Hispanics, and Women* (Washington, D.C.: U.S. Government Printing Office, 1982).

21. White House Conference, p. 13.

22. *Ibid.*, p. 12.

23. Allyson Sherman Grossman, "Working Mothers and Their Children," *Monthly Labor Review*, 104, No. 2 (May, 1981), p. 52.

24. *Ibid.*

25. White House Conference, p. 13.

8

Sex Equality, Women's Employment, and the Family

Dana V. Hiller, Ph.D.

UNIVERSITY OF CINCINNATI
CINCINNATI, OHIO

Changes in life patterns in modern society which appear to negate important family values have generated much debate. In this paper I hope (1) to clarify the ideological views that have made the family a political issue; (2) to describe the sex role division of labor through time in order to provide some perspective; (3) to discuss the causes of women's increased participation in the labor force; and (4) to discuss the implications of that employment for family life, marital solidarity and child rearing.

The liberal, democratic society of America has been truly experienced as liberal and democratic only by some people, mostly by middle class white men. To correct this situation for women will necessitate new family forms, because family stability and child rearing in recent generations have rested upon prescribed sex roles that assume different unequal opportunities for men and women. At the same time, human beings have genuine needs which have traditionally been met by the role of women in the family, including needs for homemaking, child rearing, sexual satisfaction, and stable, loving relationships. These behavioral patterns are valued no less today than in the past, but we have a new consciousness about the sacrifices women have made in meeting these needs.

As some women have sought more self-determination and control over their own lives, which is simply the human dignity the liberal society promises, others have said if women realize these things, the family and all it provides will be destroyed. Loneliness, isolation, and disintegration of the social order will follow. Consequently, the necessity of maintaining essential family functions in the traditional way is the reason offered for not pursuing sex equality.

I will suggest in this paper that the family is an *infinitely adaptable* social institution in the same way that human beings are infinitely adapt-able to newly evolving physical and social environments. No one form of the family is essential for the maintenance of social order. I will also suggest that if we cannot increasingly achieve the liberal society, including equal opportunity and basic freedoms for the individual, regardless of race or sex, we will no longer have a free and democratic social order, but rather a rigid authoritarianism. Finally, I will suggest that the concern for family and the sense of belonging it provides is also very important. Human beings do require nurture and support from others. What must occur now is the development of social arrangements that will sustain nurturing families as well as the liberal society for all people, women and men.

IDEOLOGICAL VIEWS

Ideology, as used here, refers to people's beliefs about what exists in the world and their values about what should exist. It is a worldview. Amer-ican society has been the exemplary product of the classical liberal ideology which originated with Locke and Rousseau in the seventeenth and eight-eenth centuries. American's dominate ideology can be summed up in the concept of *individualism*, which includes a strong commitment to individ-ual autonomy and independence, freedom of choice, equality of opportu-nity, and equality before the law. Feminism, basically an extention of this individualism, calls for the same tenets of classical liberalism to be applied to women as well as to men. Sex equality, then, means a dramatic change in the power structure of this society; and because any discussion of sex equality must include family matters, the family has emerged as a central political issue today.

Today's radical right, called the "New Right," is a populist movement which is explicitly anti-feminist and calls for a reassertion of patriarchal forms of the family. The underlying fear of New Right single-issue groups is that women's independence will usher in an era of immorality and social anarchy. Generally, their positions are reactionary responses to the contin-ued dissolution of the patriarchal social forms of agrarian society (Gordon and Hunter, 1977-78:12). The New Right represents those for whom pa-triarchal structures remain viable in the present and those for whom in-creased competition for the rewards of life is threatening.

The New Right tends to blame reform liberal groups for the decline of patriarchy. However, I believe it is the process of societal evolution itself that has really been responsible for this decline. Nevertheless, the New Right believes the Welfare State has taken over the functions of the family and been responsible for pulling wives into the labor force. This group believes the dominance of the patriarchal family must be reestablished to revitalize the capitalist economy and to create a moral order (Gilder, 1981). Their attack is most specifically directed at the married working woman (Eisenstein, 1982).

Married working women are definitely an approporiate target for groups who wish to defend the power structure of the status quo. The double working day and the consistently lower wages of these women highlight the fact that individualism and equal opportunity have been predominantly for men. The increasing consciousness of these inequalities on the part of married, working women has strengthened the pressure for change. Because feminists have exposed the economic and physical exploitation of women both within and outside the family, it appears that they negate traditional and positive family values. In the continued polarization of ideology, the New Right has claimed these traditional values as their own. The New Right solution for the economy and for families is that women leave the labor force and return to their altruistic activities both in the family and in the community.

The concerns of the New Right for family, in terms of the loss of services and nurturance traditionally provided by women, are authentic and serious. It is true that women's family roles and their volunteer roles in the neighborhood and community have been important integrative forces (Hiller, 1981). These concerns have not gone unnoticed by reform liberals or feminists, but concrete social structures for achieving both sex equality and fulfilling the integrative and nurturing functions women have performed have not been easy to develop (see Thorne, 1982 for a discussion of feminist ambivalence about these issues).

The crisis for post-industrial society is *not* just ideological; it is very real. Both the participation of women in the labor force and the ideology of sex equality result from a combination of social forces—economic, demographic, and cultural—which are part of the evolution of society. We could not, even if we wanted to, recreate the era in which the traditional, patriarchal family was more appropriate. Changes in family forms are likely to occur whether we abhor or embrace them.

I would like to identify three *conditions* associated with the overall crisis. First, there is the *inconsistency between American ideology and reality*. The dominant ideology—American individualism—calls for freedom of the individual and for equal opportunity. However, many people are now recognizing that the liberal, capitalist society we applaud rests substantially upon an underpaid female labor force, a significant volunteer army of women, and the absolutely essential housekeeping and child rearing work of women in families. In part the liberal society has been made possible for men because of the limited and restricted roles that have been defined for women.

Second, there is the *inconsistency within American ideology*. There is a conflict between competing sets of value, neither of which is expendable; but under present social arrangements the sets of values are incompatible. On the one hand, we recognize that meaningful interpersonal relations provide personal identity and self-worth for individuals; that these interpersonal relations grow best from stable families within a sustaining community; that what has been "women's work"—the nurturing and caring for the young and the old, the sick and the disabled, and the feeding, clothing, teaching, and serving of others—is absolutely essential to our well-being as individuals and as a society. But on the other hand, this kind of activity has not been rewarded. Our individualistic society stresses competition and achievement. It has put highest priority upon productive and creative, instrumental activities. The expressive, integrative functions have been assured by restricting women to specific roles, rather than by building a reward system that places high value upon these endeavors.

Finally, there is the real trend of *increasing individuation*. This individuation is associated with the rationalization of society, a process occurring independently from ideological considerations. In traditional societies of the past the social order was largely maintained by the strength of custom and the ascription of certain roles to individuals. Today in larger and more complex societies life is freer from coercion and obligation. Most social relations are defined by mutual agreement, by contract. Individuals have greater independence and self-reliance, and therefore greater human dignity in a society based more on rational thought than on cultural tradition. However, this fact may have profound implications for the essence of family and community (Hiller, 1981). There may be some limit at which individuation goes beyond the minimal integrative needs of society and the minimal relational needs of individual human beings. In short, since women have been the ones holding family and community together and they, too, are being liberated from ascriptive requirements, new social arrangements for seeing that the integrative tasks are completed will have to emerge. These three conditions are themselves products of the process of social change which has moved society from primitive groups to the complex, urban societies of today. Before we can look explicitly at the causes and effects of women's recent, increased labor force activity, it will be helpful to understand the change process itself by focusing first upon the change in the roles of men and women.

THE DIVISION OF LABOR BY SEX

The economic activities which people engage in to feed themselves have been the most influential patterns of behavior for shaping the rest of the social order. There have been four general types of sustenance-getting activity, and these types are based upon the tools and techniques people bring to that activity. The types are hunting and gathering, horticultural, agrarian, and industrial. In each of these, men and women have shared a division of labor; the nature of the division is a significant factor in their relative power (see Blumberg, 1978 for a discussion of sex roles and the techno-economic base).

The greatest sex equality occurred in hunting and gathering societies in which men were predominantly hunters and women predominantly gatherers, but both did a little of each of these activities. In these small, nomadic societies people lived nearer the edge of survival. They collected food daily. Although in some areas food was abundant, little surplus was accumulated. These societies were cooperative bands of people with few power or status differentials.

At some time people learned to cultivate plants and grow their own food. With this development the bands of people became more permanently settled, and women began to do more gardening than gathering. Men became warriors protecting their lands, while women did the gardening. The practice of polygamy developed in which some men had several wives who could then create a surplus of goods for their respective husbands. The power differential between men and women in society began to grow with these developments.

About 6,000 years ago when the plow was invented, fewer workers on the land could support even more people. This was the beginning of a new techno-economic base, the agrarian society. Such societies were controlled by the landowners to whom the peasants paid exploitative rents for using the land. Because children, especially sons, could help work the land and satisfy the increasing demands of the landlords, they were assets; so the population grew more rapidly. Men worked the land at this time, and women became predominantly baby-producers throughout their short life-spans. Nutrition and health care were male-oriented, and female infanticide was not uncommon. Men were the major economic producers, and women specialized in child rearing and running the domicile (Sullerot, 1971:20).

Industrial society, beginning in the early nineteenth century, brought the first major step in what some people call the liberation of women. On the one hand, industrialization provided an opportunity for less rigid sex roles by providing females with at least the opportunity to be self-sup-

porting. On the other hand, the separation of work from the home desig-
nated the great majority of married women to be housewives without direct
economic function, and this resulted in their becoming even more dependent upon their husbands. By the late nineteenth century, however,
jobs became increasingly available even for women. The opportunity to
feed oneself was at least present for those women who needed to escape
especially harsh and difficult marriages. From that time to this, sex equality
has increased both within the family and without because for women there
has been some alternative to total dependence upon men.

WOMEN'S INCREASED EMPLOYMENT
OUTSIDE THE HOME

Women's increased employment outside the home is a result of several related social forces concomitant with the developing industrial techno-
economic base. Perhaps the most important has been the needs of economic organization. The low birth rates during the depression years of the
1930s and the economic expansion after World War II combined to create
high demand for labor in the mid-twentieth century. Most recently the
demand has been specifically for female labor because the economy has
greatest need for workers in jobs traditionally held by women, namely in
the service and office occupations.

While women have been employed more often in the service occupations for which more training is necessary, men have traditionally been
the workers in the declining sectors of agriculture and manufacturing.
Technological development has caused fewer people to be employed in
agriculture and other primary industries, and in fact, in any unskilled jobs.
The effect of automation is that fewer and fewer will be employed even in
manufacturing activities.

A second reason for the increase in women's employment outside the
home is related to the dramatic change in factors affecting human reproduction. The major factors are: decline in infant mortaility, decline in fertility, and increased life expectancy.

Historically, birth and death rates were, for the most part, very similar, and there was no population growth. In agrarian societies half the ba-
bies did not live to the age of fourteen, so it was necessary to bear at least
four children in hopes that two might survive to adulthood (Sullerot, 1971:62).
The industrial revolution caused a tremendous drop in infant mortality,
largely because people were receiving more adequate nutrition. The overall result of very efficient replacement of the population meant far less of

women's time had to be spent in childbearing and child rearing. Also in industrial societies fertility has declined. The most obvious reason for the decline in fertility is that children in an urban, industrial society are economic liabilities rather than assets for their parents. They are increasingly costly to train and rear for adulthood, in contrast to an agrarian society in which children were able to produce some surplus beyond their own survival needs rather early in life. It may also be that human beings are less fertile in dense urban environments because the life-style is fast-paced and mentally stressful. I am aware of no scientific evidence for this speculation, but we do know that among most species reproduction is curtailed when creatures live in densely populated environments.

The dramatic increase in life expectancy is also important. The life expectancy at birth for American women was 55 in 1920, 65 in 1940, 73 in 1960, and 78 in 1979 (Statistical Abstracts, 1981:69). The trend involves a qualitative as well as a quantitative change because the increase includes an increase in sexual life expectation. Among women in developed countries the age of puberty is dropping and the age of menopause is receding, probably as a result of improved nutrition and hygiene. This means that years of old age are not being "tacked on," but rather the full life span is being extended (Sullerot, 1971:53-55). This is so for both sexes; however, because women have greater longevity than men and because women marry older men, more and more women will end their lives without marriage partners.

The drop in infant mortality, the concomitant drop in fertility, and the increased span of productive life have important implications for the changing nature of women's lives. A dramatically smaller percentage of the total life span of a women is necessary for child rearing activity.

These economic and demographic facts, plus the fact that women are now being educated in the same proportions as men, contribute to the inevitability that women will increasingly function in productive economic capacities. Educated women with skills to offer are likely to want to apply them. Not only would barring women from economic activity be very wasteful of human resources, but to do so would deny half the population the right of self-expression and self-actualization. An additional rationale for educating women is that they must be prepared to care for themselves at the end of their lives when they may be without male partners.

Recent employment data indicate that in 1979, 43 million women were in the United States labor force. They constitute 40% of all American workers. Of women between the ages of 18 and 64, 60% are employed, whereas the comparable figure for men is 88%. Sixty-six percent of college educated women are employed. Projections are that within another fifteen years, women's work lives will resemble those of men, and comparable proportions of the sexes will be working.

The employment of women has increased throughout the twentieth century, but the change has been most dramatic over the last twenty years. In 1960 about 38% of all women were working, compared to 52% in 1979. In 1960, of the married women with children ages 6 to 17, 39% were working, and of those with children under 6, 18% were working. Today the comparable figures are 59% and 43% respectively (Statistical Abstracts, 1980:403). Nearly half of the mothers of pre-school age children are employed.

That a large number of women are employed in economic production is not new. That has been true through the ages. Only in the more affluent families could women ever be simply decorative companions to men, home managers, or mother specialists. However, in the past, most of women's economic production was carried out within the home so it could be combined with housekeeping and supervision of children. What is new is that nearly all economic production now occurs outside the home, and this easy combination of tasks is no longer possible. The role conflict for women who need to work for income or for their own well being and who are also wives and mothers has been considerable. This dual role has raised questions about the effects of the employment of married women on families.

EFFECTS ON FAMILY LIFE

The body of empirical research about the effects of women's employment on families has grown rapidly and continues to grow. Rallings and Nye (1979) provide a thorough review of this literature through the mid-1970s. A cursory summary of their review suggests the following relationships between wife-mother employment and family variables. Employed women tend to be healthier than unemployed women, but they may experience more anxiety and/or guilt related to role expectations. An important intervening variable in this relationship is the approval of significant others in the woman's life; such as husband, parents, friends, and children. Employment for women is likely to be associated with more positive relationships with children.

Employed women spend less time in household labor and other domestic roles. They appear to have greater power in family financial matters and other external decisions. As might be expected, their husbands do more household tasks and have less overall family power than husbands of unemployed wives. The effects of wives' employment on husbands' marital satisfaction is complex and contingent upon the stage of the life cycle, the economic needs of the family, whether the wife enjoys working, and the husband's attitudes about the employment of women.

The critical research being done now is focusing upon *dual-career marriages* in which both partners have demanding jobs requiring high commitment and ego investment. Because of the considerable income differential between men and women due to the sex-segregated labor force, there are still very few dual-earner marriages in which wives are earning more income or even nearly equal income compared to their husbands. Consequently, the husband's job takes priority, and the rest of the family's activities, including the wife's employment, is contingent on the husband's interests. Scanzoni and Scanzoni (1981) call this situation the senior/junior partner marriage rather than the equal partner marriage and note that it is not very different from the traditional head/compliment marriage in which the wife is unemployed. The wife continues to be in charge of the domicile and simply adds on a paid job. The husband is likely to help a little more at home but his primary role is still seen as breadwinner. Two issues related to dual-earner and dual-career families have generated much concern. How does a wife's being employed affect marital solidarity, and how does it affect the task of child rearing?

EFFECTS ON MARITAL SOLIDARITY

The data on divorce reveal a steadily rising divorce rate since 1860. The rise in the rate is often depicted as worse than it is. In 1977 the refined divorce rate was 37 divorces for every 1000 married women. This means that under 4% of married women chose to end their marriage that year. It is also true that nearly all divorced persons remarry within five years. The longer a marriage lasts the less likely it is to be dissolved: 65% of all women whose first marriage ends in divorce are between 14 and 29, 24% between 30 and 39, and 11% over 40. It is still largely young marriages that are dissolved (Scanzoni and Scanzoni, 1981:631-636).

There is concern that the level of commitment to working out serious marital difficulties has dropped, but that is simply speculation. In traditional, agrarian society and early industrial society divorce was a rare phenomenon, but desertion was not. Divorce was expensive and something possible only for the more affluent. Much of the perceived change in marital dissolution is a result of the increasing availability of legal divorce to more people. In the past more people probably did endure unhappy marriages. Everyday life involved more sex-segregated activities so husbands and wives were not together so constantly, and extended families provided interpersonal supports when married couples did not share close emotional relationships. Today the isolated nuclear family has placed a heavy burden upon husbands and wives to be all things to each other. The expectation for a close and intimate relationship is high, at least among middle class couples. Good communication, good companionship, good sex, and having shared interests, values, and goals are part of those expectations. Juliet Mitchell (1971:14) speaks of the contradiction between the voluntary, contractual character of "marriage" and the involuntary, uncontrollable character of "love." The notion that love occurs only once in every life and can consequently be permanently integrated into a voluntary contract may be implausible, she says. Yet today we are asking love, not economic function, to carry the heaviest burden in cementing marriages.

What does dependence and the relation of wives' employment to dependence have to do with marital solidarity? Men and women have depended upon each other in complementary ways—women upon men as buffers against an alien world, and men upon women to manage their emotional domestic lives. This symbiosis has sometimes encouraged immature behavior from both partners. It has also assured males a monopoly on economic and political power (Willis, 1982:181). Some women are giving up this pejorative sense of dependence.

At least one piece of recent research suggests that two independent spouses may have a better chance for marital success. Simpson and England (1981) have posited a theory they call "role homophily." They assume that similarity of roles can build marital solidarity; that when both spouses participate at home and in the socioeconomic system, they bring similar objective interests into their marriages. The researchers studied the effects of wives' employment status upon *agreement with and understanding of spouse, marital commitment*, and *marital satisfaction* for both spouses. They found positive relationships for all three. The effects were even stronger for husbands than for wives. The basic tenet of role homophily is the opposite of the "role differentiation" theory promoted much earlier by Parsons (1942; 1955). Parsons believed role specialization was efficient and prevented status competition between spouses. Empirical work supported Parsons when he was writing, but now the norms have changed, and many more women are working. Present studies do not find wives' employment so problematic for marriages (see Oppenheimer, 1977; Hiller and Philliber, 1980). Simpson and England conclude that Parson's theory was a static conception positing a particular normative structure relating the family to the socioeconomic system; and that the subordination of wives inherent in Parsons's view actually impairs the companionship that couples now seek.

This piece of research presents a positive note about dual-earner couples. Some research is less optimistic. One study has found that the most highly educated women of all (those also likely to have the highest incomes and therefore to be most economically independent) have the highest divorce rates (Houseknecht and Spanier, 1980). Divorce and education are generally negatively related, and women with bachelors degrees have the lowest rate of all—10%. However, with one year of graduate training, that rate rises to 15%, and with two years it rises to 19%.

My own research suggests a similar theme. William Philliber and I have been studying the effects of relative job statuses of spouses for changes in marriage or wife's job (Philliber and Hiller, 1983). We found that women employed in male sex-typed managerial/professional positions and married to men of similar status are somewhat more likely than would be expected to divorce, to leave the labor force, to move to a lower status job, or to shift to a female sex-typed position. These findings seem to suggest that people are finding it difficult to cope with egalitarian marriages as those are measured by equal status or position in the socioeconomic system.

Marital strife today may in part be a result of different expectations on the part of the two spouses about their particular role bargain and/or respective statuses. This may result from change in the behavior and consciousness of women occurring before it does for men. If and when egalitarian families become the norm, I would expect marital discord not to be especially associated with the relative statuses of spouses but with more direct sources of personal conflict. However, the increased ability of some women to care for themselves economically will continue to make dissolution for those women less costly than for those who are economically dependent upon their husbands; for this reason women with the highest incomes or highest education may continue to have higher than average divorce rates for some time.

EFFECTS ON CHILD REARING

An equally critical question to ask is what will be the effects of the increase in wives' employment upon childbearing and child rearing? We have known for some time that women's employment interacts with a number of variables that affect fertility (Burr, 1973:268), and that plans of couples to have no children at all are generally related to plans for the wife's employment (Hoffman and Hoffman, 1973).

The traditional sexual division of labor, economic dependence of women upon men, and the combination of procreation with sex have provided a social structure guaranteeing the production and socialization of children (Lorber, 1975). As these social mechanisms disappear with growing sex equality, some new mechanisms in the form of institutionalized rewards and strong societal enforcements may be necessary to guarantee a replacement level of fertility and relatively stable parenting. Of course, whether even "replacement level" of fertility is necessary or desirable at this time is a different question. Nevertheless, in addition to some more radical suggestions, Judith Lorber (1975) has posited that tax-supported child allowances, expanded day care, and expanded public education will be necessary to keep families in business.

Hunt and Hunt (1982) elaborate on this theme with the suggestion that as careers become more legitimate for women, having careers and having families will become increasingly polarized. They believe the incentive to form families may have been taken too much for granted; and they point out that adding housekeeping and childcare to two demanding careers creates great logistic difficulties. So far dual-career families have not represented a radical departure from conventional sex roles. Highly educated wives have traded nonpaid, public, volunteer roles for careers of "limited ambition," and this has been made possible largely by domestic help.

The authors argue that it is *two careers*, not women's employment, that is incompatible with family life. Two distinct life-styles, centered upon careers or upon family, may evolve. Those without children will have such an advantage that they may be the pacesetters in the competition, creating a gap in standard of living and in public power between parents and non-parents. Hunt and Hunt (1982) believe the need is for a family policy which helps families survive and thrive and tempers the extremes of careerism.

These notions may underestimate the desire to form families and raise children, but current trends do not yet contradict them. They highlight the importance of having the entire society place a high value on the business of child rearing, and, more generally, on the importance of what has been considered "women's work." They highlight the concerns expressed most vociferously by the New Right but which are vital to everyone. Can and will society's value system be altered giving more attention and reward to the integrative activities in the family and the community?

THE FUTURE: IDEOLOGY AND REALITY

We face ideological dilemmas and real dilemmas. We believe in the liberal society, but we have become aware of the extent to which we have achieved it only for some groups at the expense of others. To have the liberal society become a reality for women will require, among other things, that we take a serious look at how we value the activities traditionally carried out by women. Motivations and inducements will need to be created to assure that integrative work previously done by women is performed by both women and men.

We are also coping with real and dramatic social change toward increasing individuation. While the form of households may not tell us the whole story about the kin and friendship networks of people, it is significant to note that by 1980 single person households were 22.5% of all households, and single parent families were 13% of all households. In contrast to these figures, single person households were 17% in 1970, 13.1% in 1960, and 11.9% in 1950 (Statistical Abstracts, 1981:42-46).

The forces for social change have diminished ascriptive roles and transferred many functions from the home to the marketplace. As a result, new mechanisms must emerge to help assure stable families and good parenting. More and more the glue we depend upon to keep families together and functioning is loving and rewarding personal relationships rather than economic or functional dependence. This requires that human beings be better equipped with interpersonal skills and the humanistic values necessary to make families work.

In response to the real dilemmas, at least two extreme ideologies have been promoted by different groups in society over the last few years. First, we have lived through the "me-decade" of the 1970s, a period of taking care of "number one" first, of the human potential movement, of sexual liberation, of assertiveness, and of a stress upon freedom from the concern for others to a point bordering on irresponsibility. Such extreme individualism intensifies competition and breaks down mutual and reciprocal bonds of informal exchange between people. While the liberal society is an important part of America's value system, there is probably a need, now, to temper the achievement motivation and the materialistic emphasis so central to the American way of life. These values can be accompanied by more altruistic concerns for the old and the young, the natural environment, and the comfort of community.

For every action there is reaction. The solution to the growing independence of individuals proposed by the New Right is not to redirect societal values toward priority support for families and children by urging males to take a more significant role in family life, but to return women to ascriptive duties. Women are to live vicariously, receiving their life satisfaction through their husbands and children. Irrespective of the values involved, such a reversal in the tide of human history is unlikely to occur. In 1979, the father was the sole wage earner in only 23% of all families (Statistical Abstracts, 1981:442). What, then, can we expect for families?

The perspective of this paper has been that, whatever our ideological views about family life may be, we will necessarily adapt our family forms to the changing circumstances caused by the interplay of technological, economic, and demographic social forces. At one level of analysis, that must indeed be true. At the same time, while we are less clear about the process, our ideas and actions as individuals can help shape the tide of history. We can work toward building social arrangements that express values important to us.

Institutions can be developed that meet the needs of human beings for both agency and communion, for both productive activity and supportive human relationships, in such a way that these functions are not sex-segregated. This means men and women would behave similarly as both engage in competitive and productive activities and in nurturing activities. If this occurred, both kinds of activities would be more equally valued in society. Pragmatically, first priorities must be new social arrangements that make child rearing possible for dual-earner couples. Creating quality day care for pre-school children, adapting school schedules, sharing of the family work at home, providing essential services in the marketplace, and designing living spaces to lessen the isolation of old and young are examples of such new arrangements.

In *The Third Wave*, Alvin Toffler (1980) describes how the electronic revolution may change our lives in the future; for example, by returning much work to the home and by making geographical moves less necessary. Such developments may result in knitting the family together in new ways and involving men in family life much more than they have been throughout the twentieth century. The future of the family is not devoid of hope, not even bleak. However, the family will be different from what we have known in the past. The drift of societal evolution is moving toward less differentiation in the roles and statuses of men and women. This may bring us closer to realizing our more humanitarian values and improving the quality of life for all Americans.

REFERENCES

Blumberg, Rae Lesser. 1978. *Stratification: Socioeconomic and Sexual Inequality*. Dubuque, Iowa: William C. Brown.

Burr, W.R. 1973. *Theory Construction and the Sociology of the Family*. New York: Wiley-Interscience.

Eisenstein, Zillah R. 1982. "The sexual politics of the New Right: Understanding the 'Crisis of Liberalism' for the 1980s." *Signs: Journal of Women in Culture and Society* 7:567-588.

Gilder, George. 1981. *Wealth and Poverty*. New York: Bantam Books, Inc.

Gordon, Linda and Allen Hunter. 1977-78. "Sex, family and the new right: Anti-feminism as a political force," *Radical America* 11 & 12 (November and February combined issue):9-26.

Hiller, Dana V. 1981. "Changing roles for women: Implications for community." *American Journal of Community Psychology* 108:223-240.

Hiller, Dana V. and William W. Philliber. 1980. "Necessity, compatibility and status attainment as factors in the labor force participation of married women." *Journal of Marriage and the Family* 42 (May):347-354.

Hoffman, L. W. and M. L. Hoffman. 1973. "The value of children to parents." In J. T. Fawcett (ed.), *Psychological Perspectives on Population*. New York: Basic Books.

Houseknecht, Sharon K. and Graham B. Spanier. 1980. "Marital disruption and higher education among women in the United States." *The Sociological Quarterly* 21 (Summer):375-389.

Hunt, Janet G. and Larry L. Hunt. 1982. "The dualities of careers and families: New integration or new polarizations?" *Social Problems* 29 (June):499-510.

Lorber, Judith. 1975. "Beyond equality of the sexes: The question of children." *The Family Coordinator* (October):465-72.

Mitchell, Juliet. 1971. *Woman's Estate*. New York: Vintage.

Oppenheimer, Valarie C. 1977. "The sociology of women's economic role in the family." *American Sociological Review* 42 (June):387-406.

Parsons, Talcott. 1942. "Age and sex in the social structure of the United States." *American Sociological Review* 7 (October):604-616.

———. 1955. "The American family: Its relations to personality and to the social structure." Pp. 3-33 in *Family, Socialization and Interaction Process*, T. Parsons and R. F. Bales (eds.). New York: Macmillan.

Philliber, William and Dana V. Hiller. 1983. "The relative occupational attainments of spouses and later changes in marriages and wife's career." *Journal of Marriage and the Family* 45 (February):161-170.

Rallings, E. M. and F. Juan Nye. 1979. "Wife-mother employment, family, and society." Pp. 203-226 in *Contemporary Theories about the Family: Research Based Theories* Vol 1, W. R. Burr et al. (eds.). New York: Macmillan.

Scanzoni, Letha D. and John Scanzoni. 1981. *Men, Women and Change*. New York: McGraw-Hill Book Company.

Simpson, Ida Harper and Paula Wyland. 1981. "Conjugal work roles and marital solidarity." *Journal of Family Issues* 2 (June):180-204.

Statistical Abstract of the United States. 1980 and 1981. Washington, D. C.: Bureau of the Census.

Sullerot, Evelyne. 1971. *Women, Society and Change*. New York: McGraw-Hill Book Company.

Thorne, Barrie. 1982. Chapter 1 in *Rethinking the Family*, Barrie Thorne and Marilyn Yalom (eds.). New York: Longman, Inc.

Toffler, Alvin. 1980. *The Third Wave*. New York: William Morrow.

Willis, Ellen. 1982. *Ms. Magazine* (July):181.

9

Changing Roles of Men and Women

The Emergence of Symmetrical Families

Patricia Voydanoff, Ph.D.

THE UNIVERSITY OF DAYTON
DAYTON, OHIO

Familiaris Consortio presents several values and societal goals relevant to relationships between men and women in the family. It also maps out the social conditions necessary for realizing some of these values. On the most general level, the document states that the moral basis for family life derives from "fostering the dignity and vocation of the individual persons, who achieve their fullness by sincere self-giving" (FC§22). In the context of respect for the different vocations of men and women, the document emphasizes the equal dignity and responsibility of women with men achieved through reciprocal self-giving in the family.

More specific values deal with the rights and roles of women in society and the family and of men as husbands and fathers (FC§§23, 25). Women should have access to public functions without discrimination. However, higher value is placed on the maternal and family roles of women. It is important to recognize the irreplaceable value of women's work in the home and to create social conditions favoring this work. Wives and mothers should not be compelled to work outside the home by economic necessity. If women perform public and family roles, they should be combined harmoniously (FC§23).

Emphasis is placed on the husband and father roles of men. Men should respect the equal dignity of their wives and reciprocate their wives' attentiveness, thereby developing marriage into "a very special form of personal friendship" (FC§25). The conditions limiting men's roles as fathers need to be changed so that fathers can be present in their children's lives both physically and psychologically. Fathers and mothers should share in the education of their children. Oppressive power by men is harmful and must be eliminated. The work of men should promote stability and harmony rather than be a divisive factor in family life. The document assumes that men are the major economic providers in families.

To what extent are these values likely to be realized in families with differing characteristics? We can see various patterns of values and their enactment in behavior by looking at two models of contemporary family life, traditional families and symmetrical families. These models will help us determine the family characteristics associated with the realization of values presented in the document. The models are ideal types encompassing much variation within each pattern. Variations within the models are examined in the context of the overall similarities associated with each model.

We will examine several aspects of traditional and symmetrical families. These characteristics are the crux of family life and reveal how family values are articulated and lived out in families. They include the division of labor by sex (who does what in families in terms of outside employment and family work); power and decision making in families; and the quality of family relationships as indicated by empathy, companionship, affection, satisfaction, and happiness. Following this analysis we will explore implications for the realization of the values presented in *Familiaris Consortio*.

FROM TRADITIONAL TO SYMMETRICAL FAMILIES

The work and family roles of men and women depend on the structure of work, the structure of family life, and the norms associated with work and family roles for each sex. The division of labor between husband and wife is a basic element of family structure. It determines the articulation of work and family roles and the nature and extent of husband-wife interdependence in the family. Sex role norms are a major criterion for allocating tasks and responsibilities among family members. Sex role definitions and expectations exist in all societies although their rigidity and content differ.

In the analysis of role differentiation in families, a distinction is often made between instrumental tasks and expressive tasks. Instrumental tasks include economic provision and household work. Expressive tasks involve maintaining interpersonal relationships in areas such as empathy, companionship, and affection. In the traditional family structure men are responsible for the instrumental task of economic provision while women focus more on household work and expressive tasks.

Scanzoni (1970) used this distinction to develop a model of family cohesion. This model is based on an exchange of instrumental and expressive rights and duties and the norm of reciprocity. An exchange of rights and duties between husband and wife exists on the instrumental level. Each is expected to perform the assigned instrumental duties thereby meeting the rights of the others. A satisfactory exchange on the instrumental level leads to a similar process of exchange on the expressive level. The mutual performance of expressive activities leads to marital happiness and satisfaction, producing further motivation to maintain the system, thereby leading to stability, solidarity, and cohesion.

Traditional norms prescribe that men work for pay outside the home and that women perform unpaid family duties inside the home. The division of labor associated with these norms forms the basis of the traditional exchange of instrumental rights and duties in one-earner families. The husband's work role, if he is successful, provides the financial resources necessary for the existence of stable and cohesive family life. The wife's performance of family duties sustains the ongoing activities of family life by keeping family members fed, clothed, and prepared for their outside activities. Wives are also responsible for much of the expressive activity in families, since they are the "emotional caretakers."

A second type of traditional family is becoming more common, that in which the wife is also employed outside the home. However, the pattern of role allocation in these families is still traditional. The husband is expected to be the major breadwinner with limited family responsibilities, and the wife is expected to maintain her primary responsibility to the family even though she is employed. These two subtypes of traditional families make up a large majority of American families. Married women's income contributes an average of 25 percent to the total income of their families. Most husbands and wives see women's employment as a necessary, yet supplementary, source of family income. Men in two-earner families perform about the same amount of household duties and child care as men in one-earner families.

When women are employed outside the home while maintaining their other instrumental and expressive duties, the traditional exchange relationship becomes disrupted. Many women perceive the added responsibilities as the price they must pay for the benefits obtained from outside employment; others experience overload and a sense of inequity in the exchange relationship. Increased levels of wife employment have provided the major impetus for changes in sex role norms and family role norms and family role allocation. Many women alternate outside employment with family responsibilities. These women work when they have relatively fewer family responsibilities, especially when they have no preschool children. This pattern contributes to the supplemental nature of women's employment since leaving the labor force for a period of time limits income and career progress.

Another approach to deal with changes in women's instrumental role is to develop a more symmetrical division of labor between husband and wife. Symmetrical role allocation consists of a relatively interchangeable division of labor between husband and wife in terms of both work and family activities. Husbands perform more family work and women perform more paid work role duties than in traditional families. Roles are allocated according to criteria such as ability and competence, time and availability, and perceived equity rather than according to traditional sex role norms. The rigid sex role differentiation of traditional families is replaced by a more flexible and diverse pattern of task allocation.

TRADITIONAL FAMILIES AND FAMILY VALUES

Division of Labor by Sex

Men are expected to work during their adult years from the end of schooling until retirement. Men are also expected to be major providers for their families by providing their wives and children with an adequate standard of living. Men who are unable to meet these normative expectations—that is, men with unstable or low-paying jobs—find it almost impossible to maintain a satisfactory family life. In addition, the structure and organization of men's work influences the shape and texture of family life. Time constraints and the physical separation of man's work from the home limit the nature and extent of family role performance. The physical effort and psychological involvement required by an occupation affect the amount of energy a worker has for family activities. Frequent transfers that are associated with many jobs lead to high levels of geographic mobility among families. Therefore, the traditional family's standard of living and its activity and interaction patterns are directly tied to the provider role of the husband.

In traditional families, women are responsible for household tasks and child care whether or not they are employed outside the home. Full-time homemakers spend between 40 and 70 hours per week on housework and child care. This figure is cut to about half among women who are employed fulltime. Between one-quarter and two-thirds of husbands do no housework; those who do, spend between 6 and 11 hours per week on household chores. Much of this time is spent on traditional male chores such as major repairs and yard work. Fathers spend between 20 and 60 minutes per working day and 30 minutes a day on weekends on child care activities. This is part of a total of 2 to 3 hours per day spent in the company of their children (Moore and Hofferth, 1979; Pleck, 1983). Men with employed wives generally spend no more time on family work than those men whose wives are full-time homemakers. Recently, small increases in men's family work time have been noted, irrespective of wife employment. However, the major change in time spent in family work consists of decreased time spent in housework by wives (Pleck, 1981).

Power and Decision Making

In traditional families husbands provide a large proportion of the economic resources of the family, and men in these families generally have more influence in decision making. The resource theory of marital power proposes that the power of the husband relative to the wife is related to the relative economic resources that the man provides to his family. This theory generally has been supported by research using a variety of methodological approaches. For example, men in traditional families tend to have more influence in decisions considered of greater importance to family members. Women who are employed outside the home have relatively more power than full-time homemakers. These patterns are influenced by the extent of ideological support provided by traditional sex role norms. For example, in upper-middle-class families the influence of men's provision of economic resources may be attenuated by relatively equalitarian sex role norms.

Quality of Family Relationships

Adequate performance of the provider role is crucial for family cohesion, family stability, and satisfying husband-wife and parent-child relationships in traditional families. When men do not provide sufficient resources for their families, family relations suffer. The problem derives from two sources—the lack of financial resouces and the failure of men to meet strong normative expectations. In addition, limited research suggests that those men who are most successful as providers, professionals, and managers, have relatively unsatisfying marriages. These men are relatively unavailable to their families because of psychological involvement in their work, long hours, and frequent travel. Men with middle-level incomes and occupational status may be best able to combine work and family roles, whereas those at the lower end have too few economic resources and those at the upper end have difficulty performing family roles.

The impact of wife employment on the quality of family relationships is contingent on several factors. Satisfaction in two-earner families is higher when wives work out of choice, when they are highly educated, when they like their work, and when their husbands approve of their working. Women who are homemakers by choice are as satisfied as women who are employed by choice.

Implications for Family Values

The family structure and norms associated with traditional families facilitate the realization of the document's values regarding men's and women's roles to varying degrees for different values. The major barrier to the realization of several values is the high priority placed on the man's role as provider. First, this priority restricts the performance of the husband and father roles and results in work as a divisive factor in the family. The demands associated with occupational activities limit men's physical and psychological presence in their families. When work activities consistently take precedence over family activities, husband-wife and parent-child relationships are affected in terms of quantity and quality of interaction. In order to increase men's participation in the life and education of their children, the demands of work on men's commitment and time must be diminished. Furthermore, the power which accompanies husband and father roles based on economic provision increases the tendency for men to have an "oppressive presence" in their families.

The emphasis placed on men's economic provider role also has implications for the value placed on women's work, inside and outside the home. Male dominance makes it difficult to foster equal dignity among men and women in traditional families. Ambivalence exists between equal dignity, male dominance in the family, and the value assigned to women's activities in the family. On one level, the homemaker and mother roles are imbued with "irreplaceable value"; however, their broad social value is limited by the label, "women's work." When almost half of the population is unwilling to engage in these activities, it is difficult to conceive of them as having equal dignity with the work given priority by that half, namely men's work. In addition, the lack of economic value and lack of contribution to social status limits the social value of homemaking. Lip service given to the value of homemaking is not backed up by rewards deemed valuable in society, that is, economic rewards, or social standing.

A sex-segregated occupational structure and asymmetrical boundaries between work and family roles for men and women prevent equality in the workplace and the elimination of sex discrimination. Women tend to work in occupations with low pay and little opportunity for advancement. These occupations are oriented toward women who enter and leave the labor force over the life course and have a relatively low commitment to work. To provide equal access to rewarding work for women and men, the structure of work must change or women must be able to compete on the same terms as men for jobs associated with high rewards. This competition is limited by asymmetrical boundaries between the work and family roles of men and women. Work is expected to impinge on the family life of men in traditional families while women are expected to limit work to respond to the needs of their families (Pleck, 1977). This pattern reinforces traditional sex role behavior of men and women in both work and family settings; it also limits women's participation in demanding and rewarding occupations and careers.

In many traditional families, barriers to companionship, empathy, and affection exist between husband and wife. *Familiaris Consortio* advocates that men reciprocate the attentiveness of their wives and live their marriages as a special form of personal friendship. Sex role socialization and different life experiences embedded in traditional families make this difficult for many men. They are taught to be strong and not to express feelings. Family research documents different styles of communication between men and women based on the instrumental-expressive distinction discussed earlier. Women are expected to maintain family relationships on the expressive level. When they attempt to involve men on an expressive level, many men have difficulty responding.

SYMMETRICAL FAMILIES AND FAMILY VALUES

Division of Labor by Sex

An emerging alternative to the traditional family is the "symmetrical family."The term as used by Young and Willmott (1973) refers to husband-wife relationships that are "opposite but similar."The term does not imply equality but suggests a move in that direction as compared with traditional families. It refers to a more balanced commitment to both work and family careers by husbands and wives. Symmetrical role allocation requires more accommodation to family needs by men and more accommodation to work demands by women than the traditional pattern. It implies less emphasis on sex-based role norms and patterns of differentiation since both husband and wife work outside the home, and both share in the family work. This role differentiation may be accomplished through a process referred to by Giele (1980) as crossover. Crossover is a mechanism by which men and women exchange specialized tasks. Women adopt some traditional male duties such as employment outside the home while men take on some traditional female family duties. The term does not imply that men and women do the same tasks; it only refers to a greater overlap and decreased differentiation according to traditional sex role norms.

The difference between traditional families with some role sharing and symmetrical families with extensive sharing of tasks and responsibilities is one of degree rather than kind. The major difference is one of responsibility for contributing economically to the family. In addition, in symmetrical families the husband moves beyond "helping" his wife with family work and assumes responsibility in this area. Both responsibility and task performance are more symmetrical.

Women are assuming outside employment at a faster rate than men are participating in family work. Most wife employment has supplemented the income of the husband, who is perceived as the major provider. Limited evidence suggests that women are changing their pattern of labor force participation and their level of commitment to work. More women view employment as a significant long-term commitment, something they will be involved in over their lifetime (Masnick and Bane, 1980; Scanzoni, 1978). This shift has implications for the amount of income contributed to the family by women, for the career goals and achievements of men and women, and for the texture of family life. Currently, however, even in dual-career families, women do more family work than men and wives give priority to their husbands' careers; for example, by moving much more often in response to their husbands' career opportunities. Overload is greatest among wives attempting to pursue full-time careers at a level of commitment equal to men (Pleck, 1983).

Some men are beginning to assume nontraditional work and family roles, such as having custody of children after divorce, working part time, and being househusbands, in order to participate more fully in family life and facilitate broader role participation for their wives. So far these patterns are limited to small numbers of middle-class men. The predominant role change among men is an increase in the time spent in family work within a generally traditional work-family context. A recent study by Lein (1979) examines sources of ambivalence and resistance to change among men. These traditional men acknowledge the economic contribution made to the family by their employed wives; however, they also see their own paid work as their major contribution to their families. This belief is reinforced by members of their male peer groups. In addition, some wives find it difficult to relinquish family tasks to their husbands.

Power and Decision Making

A basic characteristic of symmetrical families is their relatively egalitarian power structure. A more equal sharing of the provider role results in a more comparable contribution of economic resources to the family by husbands and wives. An outgrowth of a relatively egalitarian power structure is increased negotiation and decision making. When tasks are not allocated according to traditional sex role norms, another form of role allocation must occur. A division of labor emerges from decision making and negotiation based on criteria such as preferences, ability and competence, time and availability, and perceived equity.

Quality of Family Relationships

Using his model of family cohesion based on the exchange of instrumental and expressive rights and duties, Scanzoni (1982) suggests that the potential for cohesion is greater in two-earner families because wife employment provides additional opportunities for exchanges of instrumental rights and duties between husband and wife. If the wife also performs economic duties and the husband also performs household duties, the expanded performance of instrumental roles provides additional motivation for the husband and wife to engage in expressive activities which in turn increases marital cohesion. This model challenges Parsons's (1949, 1955) hypothesis that wife employment decreases family cohesion because role differentiation is decreased. According to Parsons, role differentiation prescribes that husbands perform instrumental roles and wives expressive roles, thereby preventing competition and increasing cohesion. The evidence is not sufficient to permit a choice between these contrasting hypotheses. Perhaps each hypothesis holds under certain conditions. For example, families with traditional sex role norms may be more cohesive when husbands and wives perform different instrumental roles.

Limited data do suggest, however, that factors associated with symmetrical family patterns are related to marital satisfaction. For example, marital satisfaction and couple enjoyment of activities are higher in dual-career families in which husbands are categorized as family-oriented rather than work-oriented (Bailyn, 1970; Rapoport, Rapoport, and Thiessen, 1974). These husbands have a more balanced commitment between work and family than traditional husbands who tend to be work-oriented. Simpson and England (1981) interpret their findings regarding marital solidarity from the perspective of role homophily theory, that is, the idea that similar roles increase companionship, common interests, and empathy. These findings contradict Parsons's role differentiation approach.

Haas's study of symmetrical families (1978), which uses a fairly strict criterion of equal responsibility in work and family roles, found several benefits and problems associated with role sharing. Family benefits include improved companionship, empathy, intimacy, flexibility, financial situation, and decision making. Increased sharing is related to individual happiness and marital happiness. Problems include the influence of traditional sex role norms on the egalitarian division of domestic chores, especially among wives, job conflicts between husband and wife, job-family conflict among individual spouses, and problems associated with housekeeping standards. She concludes that role sharing benefits couples in which both husband and wife are committed to it and she points out structural problems in achieving symmetry, including traditional sex role norms and the structure of employment.

Implications for Family Values

As in the case of traditional families, the various aspects of symmetrical families have different implications for the realization of values expressed in *Familiaris Consortio*. The decreased power differential between husbands and wives should foster a recognition of equal dignity between men and women. Respect for the differing vocations of men and women should also increase; however, the vocations of men and women would differ less. More equal sharing of, and responsibility for, family work should increase the level of respect associated with it. The perception of the irreplaceable value of family work should be increased as it is broadened to include a vocation for men as well as women. It would not be necessary to establish conditions to favor women's work at home over outside work; however, work at home should increase in status as it becomes valued for both sexes.

Symmetrical families would allow both men and women to combine their work and family roles more harmoniously if the structure of employment were also changed to facilitate family roles for both men and women. As it is now, the structure of employment limits the family participation of men and women, though differently. Men spend less time and energy with their families as they respond to the demands of work. Women limit their labor force participation to accommodate family needs thereby restricting their career development and the financial well-being of their families. Family-oriented changes in the structure of work should also reduce sex discrimination against women in the workplace.

Symmetrical family patterns would also facilitate the roles of husband

and father. Less sex role differentiation would improve husband-wife communication, thereby enabling husbands to reciprocate the attentiveness of their wives and develop their marriage as a special personal friendship. Reducing the economic burden on men would allow greater psychological and physical presence of fathers, and more egalitarian power structures would reduce the oppressive power of men in families. This, of course, assumes that sex role norms develop further so that these processes can occur. Traditional sex role norms still hinder the development of these symmetrical patterns.

Conclusion

Both traditional and symmetrical families facilitate the realization of some of the family values expressed in *Familiaris Consortio*. Traditional families emphasize the husband's provider role and the value of women's work in the home, thereby accentuating the different vocations of men and women. However, it may be difficult to assure equal respect for these vocations since the power differential between men and women, which is embedded in traditional families, limits societal rewards for women's traditional roles. This reveals an inconsistency in the values presented in the document. How can women's work be honored and sex discrimination in public roles be eliminated in the context of men's traditional power advantage?

Symmetrical families are more likely to promote harmony between work and family roles, increase equal access to public roles for women, and encourage the development of expressive aspects of husband and father roles. Symmetrical patterns currently exist in a small number of mostly middle-class American families. Scholars disagree on the likelihood that symmetrical families will become a prominent family pattern. Those with reservations point to constraining factors such as rigid work structures that limit access to family life, career penalties for those too involved in family life, and the pervasiveness of traditional sex role norms making crossovers difficult. Both men and women tend to resist changes in the allocation of family work from a traditional to a symmetrical pattern. The process of change is laden with uncertainty and ambiguity as to "who should be doing what" among families grappling with changing roles. What is an equitable exchange of rights and duties in families where both husband and wife are involved in outside employment and family life?

The structure of work, family patterns, and sex-role norms interact to influence which family values are realized in any society. For example, the development of family-oriented personnel policies and practices is hindered by normative constraints. Several of these practices have been developed from the perspective of women's desire and need to combine work and family roles while giving higher priority to famiy responsibilities. These include part-time employment, job sharing, maternity leaves, and flexitime. However, these programs are often associated with low-paying jobs, limited opportunity for advancement, and few employee benefits.

To reduce the burden on families of accommodating occupational conditions, it is necessary for these family-oriented workplace policies to be extended to, and used by, men. This requires increased recognition of the legitimacy of family responsibilities for men and the elimination of implicit career penalties associated with using family-oriented personnel practices. For example, flexibility regarding the refusal of transfers is increasing. However, after an individual has refused a certain number of transfers, there is still a tendency to question that individual's commitment to work and to limit career advancement accordingly. This example indicates the interaction between attempts to change employment policy and the tenacity of traditional attitudes toward work and family.

This paper suggests that symmetrical family patterns will not destroy family values as some have feared. The decreased difference in the vocations of men and women is outweighed by the benefits to both men and women of other values resulting from more symmetrical family and work relationships.

REFERENCES

Bailyn, Lotte. 1970. "Career and family orientations of husbands and wives in relation to marital happiness." *Human Relations* 23 (April): 97-113.

Giele, Janet Zollinger. 1980. "Crossovers: new themes in adult roles and the life cycle." Pp. 3-15 in Dorothy G. McGuigan (Ed.), *Women's Lives.* Ann Arbor: University of Michigan.

Haas, Linda. 1978. "Benefits and problems of egalitarian marriage: a study of role-sharing couples." Paper presented at the Annual Meeting of the American Sociological Association.

Lein, Laura. 1979. "Male participation in home life: impact of social supports and bread-winner responsibility on the allocation of tasks." *The Family Coordinator* 28 (October): 489-95.

Masnick, George, and Mary Jo Bane. 1980. *The Nation's Families: 1960-1990.* Cambridge, MA: Joint Center for Urban Studies of MIT and Harvard University.

Moore, Kristin A., and Hofferth, Sandra L. 1979. "Effects of women's employment on marriage: formation, stability and roles." *Marriage and Family Review* 2 (1): 27-36.

Parsons, Talcott. 1949. "The social structure of the family." Pp. 241-74 in R. N. Anshen (Ed.), *The Family: Its Function and Destiny.* New York: Harper.

———. 1955. "The American family: its relations to personality and to the social structure." Pp. 3-33 in T. Parsons and R. F. Bales (Eds.), *Family, Socialization and Interaction Process.* Glencoe, IL: The Free Press.

Pleck, Joseph H. 1977. "The work-family role system.' *Social Problems* 24 (April): 417-28.

———. 1981. "Changing patterns of work and family roles." Paper presented at the American Psychological Association, Los Angeles, August 24-28.

———. 1983. "Husbands' paid work and family roles: current research issues. In H. Z. Lopata and J. H. Pleck (Eds.), *Research on the Interweave of Social Roles*, vol. 3: *Families and Jobs.* Greenwich, CT: JAI Press.

Rapoport, Rhona, Robert Rapoport, and Victor Thiessen. 1974. "Couple symmetry and enjoyment." *Journal of Marriage and the Family*, 36 (August): 588-91.

Scanzoni, John H. 1970. *Opportunity and the Family.* New York: Free Press.

———. 1978. *Sex Roles, Women's Work, and Marital Conflict.* Lexington: Lexington Books.

———. 1982. *Sexual Bargaining.* 2d Edition. Chicago: University of Chicago.

Simpson, Ida Harper, and Paula England. 1981. "Conjugal work roles and marital solidarity." *Journal of Family Issues*, 2 (June): 180-204.

Young, Michael, and Peter Willmott. 1973. *The Symmetrical Family.* New York: Penguin Books.

PART FOUR

Family Policy

Introduction

Familiaris Consortio addresses relationships between families and society and families and the state by outlining reciprocal obligations between families and society and by proposing a charter of family rights. Families must contribute to the welfare of society and human beings by caring for others and by assuming responsibility for transforming society through political activity (FC§44). On the other hand society must foster and support families and not usurp their functions (FC§45). The charter of family rights proposes a broad range of rights that families should be able to expect from any social order (FC§46).

The papers by Harblin and Regier draw upon these principles and rights in their discussions of family policy; however, they emphasize different aspects and arrive at different conclusions. Harblin refers to the ongoing mission of creating an environment favorable to the development of family life. Actualizing the charter of family rights will contribute to a healthy societal environment for families. This actualization, in turn, requires a heightened level of consciousness about the needs and rights of families and the enactment of a comprehensive national family policy. Thus, Harblin's argument rests on the principle that society and the state must provide the conditions and aids needed by families without usurping their functions.

Regier focuses on the role of the Reagan Administration in building family strengths. This role includes promoting economic growth, targeting Federal support to those in greatest need, and limiting Federal programs to needs that cannot be met at the state level. This role has been formulated in the context of three principles: the family is the basic unit of society; the prevention of family dissolution is desirable; and programs must be oriented toward promoting family self-sufficiency.

These papers emphasize different sides of a familiar dilemma in policy analysis. What is the role of society and the state in assuring the welfare of individuals and families? To what extent are individuals and families responsible for their own well-being? At what level, federal, state, or local, should supports be provided to families in need? Obviously, both the structural and individual approaches are necessary. The document itself does a careful job of presenting this view. Harblin emphasizes the structural position while recognizing the role of families and communities. Regier focuses on local and family responsibilities without explicitly acknowledging the constraints imposed on families when national policies do not address family rights.

The second major policy element in *Familiaris Consortio* is the charter of family rights. These rights are proposed as a means of furthering the development of family life and preventing states and societies from usurping family functions. Harblin categorizes these rights as developmental, environmental, or political.

The Regier paper emphasizes the benefits from local responsibility for meeting family needs. One of these benefits is the ability of families and communities to tailor programs to local conditions. The federal role is to develop programs beyond the scope of local communities and to target programs to those in greatest need.

The issues raised in *Familiaris Consortio* and addressed by Harblin and Regier will remain in the political arena for the forseeable future. The ways in which they are resolved is of great importance for the nature and quality of family life.

10

Actualizing Family Rights

Christian Participation in the Development of National and International Society

Thomas D. Harblin, Ph.D.

UTICA COLLEGE OF SYRACUSE UNIVERSITY
UTICA, NEW YORK

Toward what end are national and international society evolving? What is the role of the family in the evolutionary process?

It is difficult to imagine positive societal and global futures that lack healthy families. Similarly, it is hard to think of positive images of family life in a degraded societal/global context. We expect well-functioning societies to foster and rely upon healthy families.

As we assess the needs and state of the family, we are led to an awareness of the value choices that are present in government policies and priorities. We must articulate family rights and exhort families and governments to implement them if we are to sustain the optimistic vision of the future to which John Paul II calls us in *Familiaris Consortio*. The nature of life on earth in the future will either be enhanced or degraded as a result of choices and policies that are now being made in the United States, the Soviet Union, and elsewhere. By serving the needs and rights of families, governments enhance the probabilities of a positive global future. A global perspective is necessary since the successful sustenance of healthy families in one society cannot be secured if it is gained at the expense of the resource base of another society's families.

In *Familiaris Consortio*, John Paul II reveals his concerns for the future of the family and national/global society. He sees these futures as clearly interdependent. John Paul II believes that to benefit families is to benefit the future, and to give greater priority to family development is to encourage the making of a more Christian national and global society.

FAMILIARIS CONSORTIO IN CONTEXT

Familiaris Consortio is an affirmation of the partnership of families everywhere. It is an exhortation to Christian families and to those in pastoral roles to undertake *concrete action* through a "special love" to "save and foster the values and requirements of the family." Our consideration of the family must start with a clear recognition of the wide-ranging *diversity* that characterizes the organization and experience of families throughout the world, particularly with regard to the highly industrialized and urbanized nations, which are economically, racially, ethnically and/or culturally heterogeneous.

The Family In a Social Context

Is the family the servant of other social institutions in modern centralized societies? Or, does the family have primacy over all other institutions? Clearly, the evolution of society entails the evolution of its component institutions. The organization and dynamics of commerce and industry change, and the organization and dynamics of family life change. To the extent that the family is less a self-contained unit of production, it depends upon the conditions of the employment marketplace to remain economically viable. The demands for a mobile, technically adaptive, low-cost labor force in an increasingly capital intensive economy help to create an environment of high employee turnover, increased female labor force participation, insecurity in family income level, and political demand for supportive welfare programs. As families respond to the employment marketplace conditions, new models of family organization and dynamics often emerge, which are assumed at first to be temporary aberrations unworthy of social legitimacy. However, increasingly these family models become more "permanent" patterns, and ultimately they become more legitimate because of their frequency. (For one illustration of how urbanization and industrialization can affect internal family dynamics in a developing nation, see: *Urbanization, Industrialization and Low-Income Family Organization in São Paulo, Brazil*. Thomas D. Harblin, Latin American Studies Program Dissertation Series, Number 48, September, 1971, Cornell University, Ithaca, New York.)

Single parent, matricentric, multigenerational, socially-isolated, casually-bonded, experimental, and so on, are adjectives which are currently used to describe the family experience of increasing numbers of adults and children. For some, these family forms provide stability, continuity, and religiously meaningful lives. For others, the same forms produce transience and alienation.

To declare, as John Paul II does, that the family has rights, implies that there are limits to which the policies of a nation pursuing its economic and political goals can be manipulative or exploitive of families. The proposed Charter of Family Rights defines those limits (FC§46).

The Mission of the Christian Family

There are two significant premises upon which the document is founded: "The future of humanity passes by way of the family"; and, history is journeying toward Christ's Kingdom of "truth and life," "holiness and grace;" "justice, love, and peace." This positive image of the future is sorely needed in a world that is shadowed by the threat and expectation of a nuclear holocaust. To John Paul II, the realization of Christ's Kingdom is intimately connected to the vitality of families. The family has "the mission to guard, reveal, and communicate love as a living reflection of, and a real sharing in, God's love for humanity."

The four general tasks of the family in carrying out this mission are:

1. To form a community of persons
2. To serve life
3. To participate in the development of society, and
4. To share in the life and mission of the Church.

Consider for a moment what the antitheses of these tasks would imply with regard to the realization of Christ's Kingdom. The antitheses are:

1. To fractionalize and alienate persons
2. To serve death
3. To participate in the destruction of society itself
4. To reject the Church

Since these are antithetical to the very idea of the Christian family per se, the centrality of the family to the realization of Christ's Kingdom can be more readily comprehended. In summary, the well-being of society is intimately tied to the good of the family.

And what is the state of families in the "modern world?" Even the modern Christian family is described as "often tempted to be discouraged and is distressed at the growth of its difficulties." On the positive side, there is "a more lively awareness of personal freedom and greater attention to the quality of interpersonal relationships in marriage." In addition, John Paul II observes that the ecclesial mission proper to the family and its responsibility for the building of a more just society have been rediscovered.

Conversely, some fundamental values have been disturbingly degraded. Mistaken notions of spousal independence and parental authority, the transmission of values, the growing number of divorces, and the scourge of abortion, are but a few of the arenas of severe value conflict.

But we are quickly reminded that the prototype and example for all Christian families, the holy family of Nazareth, underwent trials of poverty, persecution, and even exile while glorifying God in "an incomparably exalted and pure way." Therefore, let us not despair. Poor, persecuted, and/or exiled, we can be "open and generous to the needs of others" and "fulfill with joy the plan of God in their regard."

What makes the holy family of Nazareth an ideal family is not, strictly speaking, its organizational form—father, mother, child—but rather its spirit and success in glorifying God, especially under conditions of severe deprivation. As such, contemplation of this ideal is not meant to reduce the legitimacy of other diverse family forms, such as single parent families, childless couples, and certain intentional communities.

The task ahead is not a one-shot, blitz campaign. It is an enduring mission for all Christians and all people of good will with whom we are to "collaborate cordially and courageously." And, we are reminded, the Good News about the family leads us along a path which includes the Cross. So, the mission will not be an easy one.

The essential task is "to create for [the family] an environment favorable for its development." And what does such an environment look like? We must know clearly, if we are to work effectively toward attaining it.

THE IMAGERY OF A FAVORABLE FAMILY ENVIRONMENT

The environment of the family is at once internal and external to it. It is the material, relational, spiritual, and symbolic, all in interaction. Internally, prayer and the grace of the sacrament of matrimony are the key resources for a favorable environment. Externally, the issue of environment is addressed largely in terms of the realization of family rights.

Rights

Generally, the idea of "rights" only comes into focus when the state is well-enough organized to establish policies and conditions which restrict what we assume to be the inherent entitlements of a people. The primitive person in a natural setting most likely did not spend much time discussing his or her rights with others. However, such discussions did occur with the advent of civilization.

A right becomes meaningful when there are societal mechanisms that allow it to be claimed. Hence, when a right is violated, concerted action will be needed and potentially effective to claim or reclaim it. With regard to the rights of families, John Paul II reminds the Church that it has "the responsibility to openly and strongly defend the right of the family against the intolerable usurpations of society and the State."

The Charter of Family Rights

The Synod Fathers proposed a Charter of Family Rights. Their proposal is to be studied by the Holy See. The Charter thus is not yet fully or officially accepted. With this qualification, the Charter is incorporated in John Paul II's exhortation.

The fourteen rights identified in the charter can be categorized heuristically as either *developmental, environmental,* or *political.* All statements of rights are political in one sense, and these categories are not, in the strictest sense, mutually exclusive. But the following categorization can help us to think about the paths to their fullest implementation as rights.

DEVELOPMENTAL FAMILY RIGHTS

The right:
1. To establish a family and to anticipate the continuity of that family
2. To stability of the bond and the institution of marriage
3. To the intimacy of conjugal and family life
4. To procreate and to socialize the children
5. Of the elderly to a worthy life and a worthy death

ENVIRONMENTAL FAMILY RIGHTS

The right:
1. To suitable housing
2. To physical, social, political, and economic security
3. To wholesome recreation
4. To protect minors from harmful influences of drugs, pornography, and alcohol

POLITICAL FAMILY RIGHTS

The right:
1. To profess and propagate one's faith
2. To bring up children in a given religious, cultural, or family tradition
3. To expression and representation before public authorities
4. To form associations in order to fulfill the family's role
5. To emigrate in search of a better life

The *developmental* rights, namely, family establishment, procreation, socialization, intimacy, stability, and a worthy elderly existence, are the very foundation of the family as a family. A compromise on any of these rights strikes at the very heart of the family and its *raison d'etre*.

Whatever the particular organizational form of the family, the *environmental* and *political* rights serve and support the developmental rights. Housing, recreation, security, and protection from unwanted external corruptions, these enhance socialization, intimacy, stability, and the worthiness of the elderly's existence. The formation of associations, the support for free expression and representation, the respect for traditions, and the practice of faith and ultimately emigration, are often means necessary to the improvement or even basic actualization of *environmental* and *developmental* rights.

Government Policy Priorities and Conflicting Values

The predictable differentiation of family organizational forms and the increasing number of families characterized by such forms as the single parent or grandparent-headed family reflect people's struggles to cope with change and stresses induced by government policies such as those on employment, welfare benefits, and the concentration of capital. The values expressed through the priorities assigned to certain policies—for example, the economic growth of large corporations—are likely to be realized in the long run only at the expense of other values, such as family stability and continuity in child rearing. It is the starting point, the fundamental value to be emphasized, that often determines the state of the family in a nation.

The state, in most modern societies, appears willing to subordinate the family to the "needs" of other social institutions; such as, the economy, the military, and government itself. In some instances such subordination is subtle and often characterized as an "unintended consequence." An example would be the economic pressures in the United States which force many women to work. For example, the percent of American women who are married and live with their husbands and who participate in the labor force, increased from 30.5% in 1960 to 50.2% in 1980. Strikingly, the percent of such women in the labor force with children under age six increased from 18.6% in 1960 to 45% in 1980. Those women with children from six to seventeen years-of-age increased in the labor force from 39% in 1960 to 61.8% in 1980. The participation rate for women with no children under eighteen increased the least, rising from 34.7% in 1960 to 46.1% in 1980.

In other cases, such subordination is overt and planned. In China, for example, the policy of limitation on family size is backed up by coercive means of deprivation, as in the case of limiting housing space.

Even in societies where *developmental* rights may be supported by means of public policy (implicit or explicit), variations in *environmental* and *political* rights create vast differences in the family experiences of whole classes of citizens. For example, in the United States, migrant farm laborers face many and severe deprivations that seriously compromise the potential of family experience. By contrast, professional persons generally enjoy the means and rights which maximize the potentials of family experience. In the poorest of nations the extremes of family experience characterized above can also be found.

If *developmental* family rights are to be actualized to their fullest potential, then *environmental* and *political* family rights must be realized. And the reverse is valid as well. *Developmental* family rights must exist if families are to be available as a force toward enhancement of *environmental* and *political* rights. So where do we, the Church, Christian families, pastoral persons, and other persons of good will begin?

ACTUALIZING FAMILY RIGHTS

We begin with a *consciousness* of the status of family rights in our locale, in our nation, in our world. This is a matter that involves *education*—education that deals with the *specific* and the *concrete*. What is the plight of the migrant farm laborer, the Brazilian human rights advocate, the Polish labor leader, the Central American guerilla, the Middle Eastern refugee, and so forth? Since the faithful cannot wait for this information to be delivered to their doorstep, they must actively inquire about it. They must help communicate the information that is the *basis of consciousness*.

Once consciousness is attained, a next step is called for. A women's rights' advocate when asked by one of my students why she was so deeply involved, responded: "Once you have seen the light at the end of the tunnel, you can't not see it any more!"

The family experience of each of us does not take place in a vacuum.

No matter how good it may be, it is diminished by the visible suffering of others. The sixties was a decade of consciousness-raising in the United States. During the seventies many wondered (most rather silently) What do we do next? How can we actualize, on a more permanent and universal basis, rights of all kinds, including the rights of families?

A clear answer may now be emerging, but it is not yet compelling to many people, including many within all segments of the Church. An inflation rate below 10%, an unemployment rate back to 5%, or an increase in the number of homes built, neither singly nor collectively will assure those rights. Action cannot begin on a large scale without an unacceptably high human and social cost until a profound and widespread transformation is wrought. What is yet needed is a *metanoia*, a comprehensive and deep change in our very commitment to existence and to the flourishing of the future. In short, a commitment to "truth and life," "holiness and grace," "justice, love, and peace."

The foundation of this *metanoia* is a realization of the "indivisability of life." The earth is not the center of the universe, man is not the most important species, America (or the USSR, or whoever) is not the greatest culture to ever exist, and each of us is truly only one momentarily living element in the human experiment. This does not mean that each of us is of no real value; nor that America is less than a good place to be; nor that humans are anything less than a beautiful version of the "one true species," namely life on earth; nor that the earth is other than an especially gifted synergy of matter and energy.

DEVELOPING A NATIONAL POLICY ON THE FAMILY

In response to the question what do we do next to facilitate family rights, I add to the call to *consciousness* and *metanoia* the suggestion that Christians in America organize to support the establishment of a concrete, comprehensive, national policy on the family. Such a policy should be developed in positive terms to set the tone and guide resource allocation.

At present, the United States does not have an explicit national policy on the family, and we have resisted developing any such comprehensive policy despite repeated efforts by family specialists to present such a policy to the Congress. For example, in 1973 hearings were held in the U.S. Senate. These were entitled "The American Family: Trends and Pressures." Abundant and revealing testimony was provided by a wide range of family life specialists and advocates. Included among that testimony was a proposed set of principles and provisions called *The American Family Act of 1974*, offered by Dr. Urie Bronfenbrenner. A copy of that proposed Act is appended to this paper. The Act identifies a series of Family Support Systems including:

1. Revision of welfare and work legislation
2. Incentive programs
3. Family impact assessment
4. Homemaker services
5. Group day care
6. Training programs for child care workers
7. Study commissions for children and families
8. Research
9. A family-centered employment policy in the federal government

The senator who chaired the Subcommittee on Children and Youth which held the hearings was Walter Mondale. In all fairness, I do not know the outcome or follow-up of those hearings. But neither am I aware that we are officially any closer to recognizing the need of American families through the development of a national family policy.

Research over the past three decades shows consistently that the developmental antecedents of behavioral disorders and social pathology are rooted in *family disorganization*. We also know that this disorganization does not arise primarily from within the family itself (that is, from "inadequate human beings"), but largely from the total environmental circumstances in which the family finds itself.

Researchers, such as Dr. Bronfenbrenner, tell us that we have the knowledge and know-how, and even considerable successful experience in applying that know-how, to increase significantly the ability and competence, and I would add, the humaneness, of the next generation of children to be born in this country. So why don't we do it?

The failure, it seems, lies largely at the level of *federal policy* and *federal action*.

Hence, establishment of a national policy on the family and its implementation should be at the top of our political agenda as Christian advocates of family rights. Such a focus at the federal level is not inconsistent with the present emphasis on the decentralization of government. We need a federal/national policy to set the tone and guide local action. We need, in Rene Dubos's terminology, to "think globally and act locally." We need to help implement a national policy that is effective in serving families in our neighborhoods and parishes. Such a policy should reinforce family rights and values in the families around us; otherwise it would be a failure. But taking the initiative here at home does not preclude our concern and action in those cases where family rights are violated or non-existent abroad. In fact, a domestic effort in America would surely support similar efforts on the international front.

Consistent with the Preamble of the Constitution, it is a proper role of our government at every level to facilitate the realization of family rights and values.

Beyond a National Policy on the Family

Frankly, even the development of a National Family Policy will not suffice to secure the family rights and values that John Paul II presents to us.

The family exists in a complex socio-cultural context. We need to understand how our very way of life puts families everywhere in a bind. Americans are about 5½% of the world's population, and yet as a people we consume anywhere from 30% to 50% of the annual flow of nonrenewable resources (energy, minerals, etc.) consumed worldwide. This severely disproportionate amount of the world's resources consumed in the United States is directly connected to the plight of families in other nations. This is a most challenging dilemma, since our very economic system depends upon, and promotes growth in, such consumption. Therefore, I believe that it is urgent for us as a nation to begin a very serious debate regarding the future of our economic system. The principal questions guiding this debate should be, What would it mean if we were to pursue actively the development of a *sustainable*, or maybe a *planned negative growth*, economy toward reducing the proportional level of our annual resource consumption? How can this be accomplished so as to minimize the trauma of adjustment for all concerned? How much is enough? (We seem to lack a clear concept of *sufficiency* regarding resource consumption.)

Addressing these questions will inevitably lead us to ask, How can we share our resources more justly? Can we afford our current and projected consumption of military/defense goods and services? And at what human and social costs are we willing to sustain such budgets?

In short, as a nation we need to go, consciously, on a *resource consumption budget*.

It is just this kind of debate that I believe the Holy Father calls us to in *Familiaris Consortio*. Christian families can introduce these questions to each other in parishes, in Catholic educational institutions, and in their local political arenas.

OBSTACLES AND PITFALLS

On our way to a national policy on the family we can easily get derailed by reducing complexity to a single, apparently clear issue. I am unalterably opposed to abortion, and yet the economic and military policies of some candidates who share my views on abortion are nothing other than "death dealing" on a massive, if at times subtle, scale. In order to avoid trading off one source of mega-death against another in choosing political candidates, people must work to promote local as well as national candidates who understand the complexities of the issues and yet who are across-the-board supporters of Life on Earth. To be opposed to abortion, but be willing to accept concepts such as nuclear deterrence, economic growth at all costs, or the death penalty, strikes me as contradictory. Such a stand defeats our purpose, which is to create a humane family environment everywhere.

Summary and Conclusion

There are five main points to the path I have laid out. They would take us much closer to actualizing family rights and values, and to "familiaris consortio," a "partnership of families." Let us:

1. Recognize and respect the *diversity* of families
2. Develop our *consciousness* of the status of family rights
3. Pursue a *metanoia* in our commitment to the future of life on earth
4. Work to establish a *national policy on the family*
5. Engage in *debate about* reducing our national level of *resource consumption*

Each of the above, as a means to a partnership of families based upon family rights and values, should be carried out with a positive, humane, and generous spirit. The stakes are high. Our Holy Father tells us that the realization of Christ's Kingdom depends upon the Christian family. Let's get on with the task.

REFERENCES

All quotes are from *The Role of the Christian Family in the Modern World*, an Apostolic Exhortation of His Holiness Pope John Paul II, St. Paul Editions, Undated.

The American Family Act of 1974 and the Congresional testimony referred to can be found in the *Congressional Record*, Proceedings and Debates of the 93d Congress, First Session, Vol. 119, Washington, Wednesday, September 26, 1973, No. 142.

APPENDIX

The American Family Act of 1974
Suggested Principles and Provisions

PROPOSED TO THE 93D CONGRESS, FIRST SESSION, BY
DR. URIE BRONFENBRENNER. REPRINTED WITH PERMISSION.

A. PRINCIPLES

1. The family is the most humane, effective, and economical system of child care known to man. *The first aim of any child care program, therefore, should be to strengthen the family and enable the parents to function as parents for their children.* This can best be accomplished by providing a variety of support systems for the family in the home, neighborhood, place of work, and community.

2. *All programs should be family-centered rather than merely child-centered.* This means service to parents as well as to children, and opportunity for the involvement of parents in the planning and execution of programs both within and outside the home. Research results indicate that where programs have involved *families as a whole* there is greater likelihood of lasting effect beyond the duration of the program itself, with an impact not only on the target child but on other children in the family as well. *Also such programs tend to be more economical because of the greater participation of family members in the work of the program.*

3. During the first six years of life, particularly during the first three, an enduring one-to-one relationship is especially important for the child's development. For this reason, special encouragement should be given to arrangements which permit one of the two parents to *work part time.* In particular, welfare eligibility requirements should not discriminate against families in which one or both parents are working part time rather than full time.

4. Many families today are unable to function effectively to meet the needs of their children because of circumstances beyond their control. *The principal debilitating factor is poverty.* Other factors include reduction of the family to only two adults, or, in many instances, only a single parent; the involvement of both parents in full-time jobs; working on different shifts; the social isolation of families—especially the mother—because of the breakdown of neighborhoods. Measures designed to alleviate these conditions can contribute to reenabling parents to function more effectively. Hence such measures should become a part of any comprehensive child

care program, especially because they are more economical in the long run.

5. In addition to the parents, other persons can play a significant role both in relation to the child himself and in providing support to those primarily engaged in his care, especially to the mother. The most important persons in this regard are other family members such as grandparents, aunts, uncles, older brothers and sisters but also neighbors, friends, teachers, social workers, and other professionals. Finally, the research evidence also points to the powerful impact of older children on the development of the young. *Therefore, both on psychological and economic grounds, an effective child care program should utilize and encourage the involvement of other adults and older children in the care of the young.*

6. To be effective, programs must be *comprehensive* in nature not only in relation to the needs of the child but also those of his family in the areas of *health, education,* and *social services.* For example, the most effective and economical measure to insure the health of the child may often be to meet the health problems of his parents, or of other sick, handicapped, or aged family members who sap the parents' strength and resources.

7. Families live in widely differing circumstances. Any program of child care services must therefore supply a *variety of options.* In accordance with this principle, *child care* services should not be limited to group day care provided outside the home.

B. FAMILY SUPPORT SYSTEMS

1. *Revision of Welfare and Work Legislation. No single parent of young children should be forced to work full time or more to provide an income at or below the poverty one.* The statement applies with equal force to families in which both parents are compelled to work full time or longer to maintain a minimal subsistence level. Under such circumstances, a parent, wishing to do so should be enabled to remain at home for part of the day. The following measures could help achieve this objective.

a. *Welfare legislation* should be amended so as to encourage rather than penalize low-income parents, especially single parents, who wish to work only part time in order to be able themselves to care for their own children.

b. To free parents in poverty from full-time employment so that one of them can care for the children, federal and state programs should provide funds for part-time parental child care at home in lieu of wages.

c. There should be legal prohibition against unlimited compulsory overtime for parents with young children.

d. *Federal or state legislatures* should pass *Fair Part-Time Employment Practices Acts prohibiting discrimination in job opportunity, rate of pay, seniority, fringe benefits and job status for parents who seek or are engaged in part-time employment.*

2. *Incentive Programs*

a. *Tax incentives* should be extended to businesses and industries who set up family and child services for their employees such as day care programs, part-time work opportunities, flexible working hours, special programs designed to acquaint children and young people with the world of work, etc. In particular, employers should be encouraged through tax benefits to modify work schedules so as to enable parents to be home when their children return from preschool or school, thus decreasing the need for baby-sitters during the child's waking hours or for "latchkey" arrangements for older children.

b. Special incentives should be provided for the development of neighborhood and community-wide programs benefiting families and children especially on a non-age-segregated basis.

c. Incentives should be offfered to groups responsible for the design of neighborhoods, housing projects, apartment complexes, churches, industrial sites, urban renewal projects, etc. to provide for the needs of children and families *in the planning of these environments.* For example, apartment complexes should incorporate day care facilities adapted for parent participation; large housing projects should be provided with a family neighborhood center.

d. Incentives should be offered to schools for introducing programs involving older children in responsibility for the young both within the school and in neighborhood settings (including the old and the sick) and also for the development of programs which bring members of the community in contact with school children so as to reduce the widening gap between the worlds of childhood and adolescence on the one hand, and the world of adults on the other.

3. *Family Impact Assessment*

Both Houses of Congress and analogous governmental bodies at state and local levels should charge or establish committees to monitor all legislation or proposals coming before the body in question for possible impact in the welfare of families and children.

4. *Homemaker Services*

Many disadvantaged or single parents are unable to spend time in activities with their young children because of other demands in the home, such as care of old or sick relatives, meeting the needs of a large family, housekeeping under difficult conditions, etc. Local residents trained as homemakers, or high school students in special programs (see above) could take over some of these responsibilities during regular visits so that the parent could be free to engage in activities with the younger child.

5. *Group Day Care*

a. Day care eligibility should not be limited to parents engaged in full-time employment.

b. Some off-hour and around-the-clock day care should be available.

c. Some provisions should be made for the availability of emergency day care when parents are sick, incapacitated, or for other urgent reasons temporarily unable to provide adequate care for their children.

d. In the establishment of care programs, provisions should be made for the *involvement of other family members besides the parents, such as adult relatives and older children of the family.*

6. *Training Programs for Child Care Workers*

These should be available for persons of all ages by including them in the curricula of high schools, adult education programs, community collegs, etc. They should incorporate as a regular feature voluntary child care services while in the period of training. This would make available large numbers of trained personnel at low-cost for families who need such assistance.

7. *Commissions for Children and Families*

Federal encouragement should be given for the establishment of such commissions *at the neighborhood or community level.* They would have as their initial charge finding out what the community is doing for its children and their families. The commission would examine the adequacy of existing programs such as maternal and child health services, family planning clinics, day care facilities, social service and recreational opportunities. They also would have the responsibility for looking at the entire community as an environment for children. Attention would be given not only to institutions and programs designed explicitly to serve families and children, but also to town planning, housing, traffic, entertainment, etc. from the point of view of meeting the needs of families and their children. The commission would be expected to report its findings and recommendations to appropriate executive bodies and to the public at large through the mass media. After completing the intitial assessment phase, the commission would assume continued responsibility for developing and monitoring programs to implement its recommendations.

8. *Research*

Provisions should be made for studies designed to *assess the comparative effectiveness of special strategies for furthering the development of children and families.* Unlike the massive surveys employed to date, such investigations should focus on specific components of particular programs, rather than attempting an indiscriminate evaluation of many complex programs differing in content, clientele, and social setting.

9. *A Family-Centered Employment Policy in the Federal Government*
The Federal Government as an employer should be mandated to set an example by adopting, at least on an experimental basis, the policies and practices proposed in these recommendations.

(Emphases throughout are mine. T.H.)

11

Public Policy for Building Family Strengths

Jerry Regier

ASSOCIATE COMMISSIONER/ACYF
DIRECTOR, FAMILY AND YOUTH SERVICES BUREAU

We are all aware that the family is a tapestry interwoven with sharing and caring; a fabric made of the threads of marital responsibility, kinship, and love. It is within the family that we learn charity, friendship, self-control, responsibility, health, discipline, and good manners. Within the family we come to understand the proper use of leisure, the development of our natural talents, the value of sincerity, perseverence, and love of country. We know that not all families are equally successful in all of these endeavors.

President Reagan said recently, "Rebuilding America begins with restoring family strength and preserving family values." This is fundamental to a revitalized America. We need to restore family strengths and preserve family values partly because of the ever-increasing role the federal government has played in the lives of families over the past twenty years.

The Reagan administration has made a fundamental departure from past administrations in the conceptualization of the federal government role in regard to social services. For decades the trend has been to assign to the federal government an ever-expanding responsibility for identifying the needs for social services and then planning, funding, and monitoring programs to meet those needs. Most frequently the needs and program responses were organized around special populations. In the past two decades we have witnessed a rapid expansion of the federal role and federal expenditures for social services and the proliferation of categorical approaches. Between 1950 and 1980, federal social welfare spending jumped from $20 billion to $300 billion. That is a fifteen-fold increase, an increase that has been seven times greater than the rate of inflation during that period. However, we are currently taking a different road.

161

This administration is committed to achieving three goals regarding federal interaction with families and the institutions that affect them:

1. Expanding state and local responsibility for all facets of planning and implementing social services while simultaneously reducing the federal role. This is the essence of the New Federalism. As part of this strategy, the administration is utilizing a block grant approach which provides state and local decision makers the flexibility to continue the categorical approaches of the past, or as they seem to prefer, to develop new consolidated approaches to meet social service needs. This consolidated approach also allows for the development of a more wholistic family focus;

2. Ensuring that the formulation and implementation of social service legislation and programs are based upon the principle that the well-being of the public is primarily a responsibility of individuals, families, and the communities in which they live;

3. Promoting the concept that when social services are needed, they are best defined and administered through public or private institutions at the level closest to the problem—state and local governments, area agencies, and local community-based and private voluntary organizations.

The role of the federal government in meeting social service needs then becomes:

1. To adopt and implement national policies or programs aimed at *promoting economic growth and prosperity* and thereby reducing the need for social services;

2. To *target federal budgetary support* toward those most in need;

3. To *address those social service needs that cannot be implemented at the state level* and that require interstate or national orientation for effective operation. The federal government will not abandon its leadership role in such important areas as child abuse, child welfare, and services for the aging and developmentally disabled.

It may be somewhat surprising that our top priority in relation to social services is to adopt policies and programs aimed at promoting economic growth. I believe that it is economic growth within the free enterprise system that creates real job opportunities that allow individuals and families to become and remain economically and socially self-sufficient. In the process, economic growth reduces the size of the poverty population and the need for, and costs associated with, social services. Economic growth, therefore, is both a remedial and a preventive strategy that will benefit many millions of needy American families.

With our three goals in mind, what are the principles that will guide us as public policymakers seeking to enhance the role of individuals and families? I would like to enumerate three which I believe form a fundamental approach to building family strengths—whether from a federal perspective or a community perspective.

1. THE FAMILY IS THE PRIMARY SOCIAL UNIT OF OUR SOCIETY

We already know and recognize the importance of the family to each of us as individuals; we also recognize the essential functions performed for society by the family. The family performs the *vital* role of developing the next generation. Therefore, we see the family as an essential unit of society and not just as an economic unit. This is an important distinction to make as we come to the policy table because as an essential unit of society the family carries great responsibility for the orderly functioning of that society and for the formation of moral values within that society. Furthermore, families are the responsibility of parents as individuals and as partners. We cannot delegate this task of keeping families strong. We as parents are responsible. We cannot abdicate our responsibilities to the school, to the church, or to the government. We certainly can turn to these institutions to assist us in fulfilling our responsibilities, but we can not relinquish our duty.

2. PREVENTION OF FAMILY DISSOLUTION IS DESIRABLE

In the past decade alone, there has been a doubling of single-parent families; such families now constitute 20 percent of all families with children. More than half of these families are poor or near poor. Ninety percent are headed by women.

We know that family dissolution forces many people into poverty. If it were not for family instability, poverty would be substantially reduced. There are certainly other factors; however, *this* fact must be addressed.

Census Bureau figures suggest that when a father, for instance, leaves his family, he often leaves his wife and children without financial support. He knows that if he abandons the family and they become impoverished, the government will take over the responsibility of providing for his family.

Only two-fifths of single-parent families headed by women receive child support payments from the father. And only 7 percent of never-married women with children receive such support from the father. On the other hand, one-half of all families headed by women receive some form of public assistance. Thus, the single-parent family is the most significant factor in the nation's current poverty figures. This lack of commitment and responsibility on the part of absent fathers is all too common today. If we sincerely desire to prevent family dissolution, then we as a government and as a nation need to foster a rekindling of commitment and parental responsibility expressed in child rearing and in marriage.

We are seeing some positive signs. Contrary to our national sense concerning this subject, the majority of marriages *do not* end in divorce or separation. A recent Gallup Poll reveals the following: 79 percent are "highly satisfied" with their family lives; 80 percent rank their family life as more important than their personal satisfaction and income. In another survey 66 percent said they were "very happy" with their marriages. The National Center for Health Statistics has reported that in 1982 the first decline in divorces in twenty years occurred.

Because of the possible effects upon our children as well as our marriages we must, as parents, express commitment to one another...and work at it. I believe there are many things I can do for my family—but the greatest single thing I can do for my four children is to love their mother.

Now, lest I be misunderstood, I also recognize the realities of our world; and when family dissolution does take place we must be supportive and not judgmental. Children in single parent families may be better off than those in families with marital disharmony; however, that is not a reason to encourage family dissolution.

3. PROMOTION OF FAMILY SELF-SUFFICIENCY AND INDEPENDENCE MUST BE THE GOAL OF OUR PROGRAMS

While we strive to prevent family dissolution, we do recognize that there are many families in need. The federal government must continue to be a factor in meeting the needs of poor families, broken families, and adolescent-headed families; families with problems of child abuse, runaway youth, disabled members, or aging and frail extended family members. Yes, services, assistance, and support must be given, but with what goal in mind? As these services are given, encouragement and skills for self-sufficiency and independent living must also be given. The necessary grassroots support networks should be organized so that families can prepare to meet their own needs and prevent the reoccurrence of problems within their power to control.

Public Policy Strategy for Building Family Strengths

What then are we doing to build upon these principles through public policy to strengthen families? Let me articulate some directions we are taking through our new "Families Initiative."

First: we are developing a pubic awareness campaign to build on family strengths and values. Working together with public, private, voluntary organizations, we believe we can promote a positive national attitude that is based upon family strengths rather than family weaknesses.

We can wage this campaign at several levels. The first level is to promote a positive national attitude that is based on family strengths rather than weaknesses; that concerns the value of the family to our society; and that focuses on the responsibility of the family as the primary developer of children. The second level is to create linkages at the local community level to communicate where the needs and resources are, in order to support families.

Let me share with you an example from the public sector of a family-focused effort which incorporates many of the principles we have discussed. This administration and Dorcas Hardy, the assistant secretary for the Office of Human Development Services, are focusing national attention on the problem of 50,000 older, minority, and handicapped children who are in foster care and institutions and are legally available for adoption. Their handicaps may be physical or emotional. Many of you have met such children. They all need permanent, loving homes.

Public Law 96-272, the Child Welfare and Adoption Assistance Act of 1980, provides support to states for subsidized adoptions of these children. We have written to the directors of each state's child welfare program encouraging greater emphasis upon adoption of these children. And we have also communicated with the governors to seek their cooperation. I believe that we need to use all our combined energy to see that these special children move out of foster care into special loving, caring, permanent homes.

There are many successful "special needs" adoption efforts in all parts of the country. In Chicago, Father George Clements, a black Catholic priest and adoptive father, has established the "one church, one child" program. In less than two years, fourteen churches have been successful in placing thirty-five special needs children in permanent homes. In New York the Pfizer Corporation, a major pharmaceutical firm, helps its employees adopt special needs children through an extensive employee benefits package. And in St. Louis, Denver, San Francisco—in fact, in about sixty cities—special TV programs seek to publicize the availability of children in need of a loving family. Agencies working with these stations report a placement rate of more than eighty percent. KRON-TV in San Francisco had six hundred calls for the first sixteen children featured. Several weeks ago I saw one of these children, an eleven-year-old boy, as a TV newscaster asked him what he was looking for in a home. He said, "I just want a mom I can call my own, and she can call me her own." You see it's personal. Governments do not adopt children; individuals and couples do.

Second: our public policy strategy for building family strengths is to ensure a family focus to the federal programs that serve our vulnerable populations. Programs like Head Start already have a strong family focus through the Parent Involvement Component. The availability of parent education through the "Exploring Parenting" curriculum is a key factor in serving the whole family rather than just the child. Through this avenue parents are learning communication skills of vital importance to successful parenting and to building family strengths. The use of this curriculum as well as other family life materials can be expanded so that many of these parents can be assisted toward social and economic self-sufficiency.

We recognize that in order to support the family in meeting its responsibility we must enhance the role of parents in our social service programs. Only as our public policies reflect this strengthening of the parental role can we truly support the primacy of the family in our society. This enhancement takes the form of increased involvement of parents in services affecting their children as well as support for parents as the primary providers and caretakers for their families. We will work toward empowering parents through their recognition of their own capabilities and competence.

Third: we will continue to assess existing policies and regulations through a family lens. What policies discourage the maintenance of the family unit? What policies do not support prevention?

Fourth: our strategy is to continue to promote public/private/community partnerships in order to build family strengths. In the past, government has crowded out many voluntary partnerships. Twenty years ago the federal government's share of spending for social services was only 6% of the national total. The state and local government share was about 34%, and the private share—the majority—was 60%. Today the federal share has increased to 38%, state and local share remains nearly the same at 32%, and the private share has declined one half—to about 30%.

Voluntarism has great historical importance in our country and the

Reagan administration is seeking an even greater role for the American volunteer spirit. We *are* looking for a new partnership with the private and volunteer sectors. We *are* looking for innovative and affordable new ideas that can be of benefit to every American. We want to create conditions in which government, the private sector, and voluntary organizations can work together to achieve goals that government could never achieve on its own, no matter how much money we spent.

We have made a beginning. One example is the cooperation that is being achieved in the area of corporate options for working families, particularly concerning child care. We explored corporate views through seminars coordinated by the Conference Board. Now, in cooperation with the White House Office of Private Sector Initiatives, we are encouraging further activities in employer-sponsored child care and family supports.

Fifth: our strategy is to encourage broader dissemination of information to parents and families. Perhaps as part of a national awareness campaign, families could be made aware of information and resources available and how to reach these resources. We are particularly concerned that vulnerable families and families at risk have access not only to materials, of which there is great abundance, but also to models. One idea might be to have Adopt-A-Family programs in the community, much on the order of Big Brother/Big Sister programs. Families have so much to share and to give. Every family has strengths it can build on as well as strengths they can share with others. We need to communicate these strengths within each of our communities in such a way as to foster an attitude of We can do it.

Conclusion

I am optimistic for America's families because of a new spirit of partnership and teamwork. I coach a Little League Team and it is a challenge each year to see how these young individuals develop into a team. It is exciting to observe as well as to be a part of the team spirit that develops.

In the same way we are a team—those in the private sector and those of us in the federal government. People in the private sector are mobilizing hundreds of communities across America. It is exciting to see. Their creativeness and innovativeness, learned and applied at the local level, can stimulate us at the federal level to be responsive in our policies so that families and their strengths are enhanced. In turn our public policy stance and direction can continue to foster new partnerships. We look forward to continuing to work together as a team.

PART FIVE

Conclusions

12

The Family in Social-Historical Perspective

Theo J. Majka, Ph.D.

THE UNIVERSITY OF DAYTON
DAYTON, OHIO

The "family" has recently become a topic for intense concern and discussion among church officials and church members, theologians, social scientists, popular writers, journalists, and others. The attention paid to the institution of the family by the 1980 Synod of Bishops in Rome and especially the publication of *The Apostolic Exhortation on the Family* in 1981 symbolized the increased concern of Catholics about contemporary changes in family patterns. Social scientists have been no less interested, as intimacy, marriage, and family studies have become areas on the cutting edge of sociology, psychology, and, to a lesser extent, history.

Why has this happened? Also, why at this point in history? It is crucial to keep in mind that this contemporary concern stems from changes in intimate relationships, sexuality, marital bonds, and family patterns that have been occurring for centuries. These changes in turn reflect substantial changes in other spheres—especially changes in the economy, cultural values, the occupational structure, and demographic patterns.

The papal exhortation covered much broader areas than did the papers and discussion at the family symposium at the University of Dayton. Pope John Paul II was not only concerned with families in Western societies but also with the very different problems facing families in underdeveloped nations and those living under politically repressive governments. Little attention was given these topics at the symposium. Instead, the focus was clearly on families in Western societies. For theologians at the symposium, the emphasis was on the facilitation of marital and familial relations as a means of fulfillment, enrichment, and contribution to spiritual experience and growth. For social scientists, the concern was to discover the sources and meaning of contemporary changes in family patterns and analyze how these facilitate or inhibit the potential for families to serve as the context for satisfactory relationships.

Characteristics of the family were given differential attention. Especially in the Family Symposium, primary attention was given to the relationship between spouses. Other areas were given little attention, such as the family's procreative function, the socialization of children, and the family's economic function. Had the symposium been held ten or twelve years earlier, a primary topic would undoubtedly have been the relationship between parents and children, due to the common public preoccupation at that time with what was perceived as a "generation gap." Instead, the absence of such discussions implies that these areas were not seen as problematic, or at least of lesser importance than marital relationships.

The reason for the focus on spousal relationships is that there have been especially rapid changes in patterns of intimate relationships during the past fifteen years. These changes, as Dana Hiller points out in her paper, are part of long-term structural changes in Western societies and are not of recent origin. The pope recognizes the reactive nature of the family at the beginning of the exhortation: "The family in the modern world, as much as and perhaps more than any other institution, has been beset by the many profound and rapid changes that have affected society and culture" (FC§1). Recent events, such as the women's movement, growth of a critical intelligentsia, development of certain themes in contemporary theology, and the effects of ten years of economic recession/depression may have stimulated particularly rapid changes in family patterns, but the structural basis for these changes has been set before. Papal concern with certain trends is evident: cohabitation, trial marriages, rising divorce rates, single parent families, and similar patterns. These patterns cut across religion, nationality (at least among Western nations), and, to a lesser extent, social class. The pope also recognizes the contribution of the social sciences to the analysis of these patterns: "The church values sociological and statistical research when it proves helpful in understanding the historical context in which pastoral action has to be developed and when it leads to a better understanding of the truth" (FC§5). The social scientists attending the symposium took this injunction seriously. In this paper, I will try to summarize the conclusions of research on the family relevant for the questions raised by the papal exhortation that have not been dealt with previously in this volume. Also, I will try to synthesize certain themes that were expressed in several of the papers.

THE MYTH OF "THE GOLDEN AGE"
OF THE FAMILY

There is a widespread belief that contemporary changes in family patterns indicate a decline in the importance and vitality of the family as a social institution. This argument comes in a number of variations, but a common theme is that the family at one time was much stronger and more harmonious and stable than it is today. Recent changes have seriously weakened the ability of the family to transmit values from one generation to the next or to serve as a source of emotional support and satisfaction to its members. Often the sources of such a decline are said to be the increasing intrusion of government policies and agencies into functions that used to be performed within the confines of a family (*see* Lasch, 1977; Donzelot, 1979; Foucault, 1981). Others point to changes in women's behavior and attitudes. The latter approach is most often associated with the Moral Majority and the "New Right," both of whom seem to feel that family life and sexual equality are incompatible.

In order for the present decade to constitute an age of family decline, there must have been some time in the past when the family was stronger, a "golden age" that we have lost. For some, the decade of the 1950s was such a time; for others, it was the 1930s, represented perhaps by the popular television program "The Waltons." For many, however, the pre-industrial family epitomized an ideal. There is a widespread perception that prior to industrialization, the family was deeply rooted in a broad set of kinship relations (the extended family) and was itself the center of economic production. Families were large, relations between its members were warm and close, and the family was the basic unit of Western societies. This picture represented an ideal of family relations based on economic production and affectionate personal ites. The breakdown of this family form, however, began even before the industrial revolution when the expansion of capitalist agriculture and enterprise undermined the family's economic function by creating, and then absorbing family members, into separate labor markets. This separation of the home and the workplace diffused individual loyalties and ultimately undermined the close-knit quality of family life.

Recent research by family historians and others suggests that this idealized conception of the pre-industrial family (sixteenth to nineteenth centuries in Europe, seventeenth to eighteenth centuries in the United States) needs substantial alteration. Although family structures preceding industrialization exhibited a wide variation, we can reach some tentative conclusions from a comparison of actual pre-industrial family patterns with the idealized perception of them as well as with patterns of contemporary families. First, it is safe to conclude that in many small-scale, non-literate societies, the family and kinship relations in general were the basic organizing principles of social life. The family, often composed of an extended family, was a primary productive unit. Production was carried on in the home or on the land adjacent to it. All capable family members, including children, made contributions to productive activity.

However, in actual living arrangements, pre-industrial families were closer to a nuclear than extended form. Despite the belief that members of an extended family all lived in the same domicile, historical research in Britain and the United States has suggested otherwise. In his study of family size and composition in pre-industrial England, Peter Laslett (1972), a Cambridge professor and perhaps the best-known historian of the family, has found that between the years 1564 and 1821 only about 10 percent of households contained kin beyond the nuclear family at any one point in time, the identical percentage for England in 1966. Evidence from the United States presents a similar conclusion. Even though it is likely that extended family living patterns were more acceptable, this did not result in a high proportion of extended families in the same household. One reason is that many people in pre-industrial England and the United States married relatively late and the life expectancy was relatively short. On the average, there were only a few years between the marriage of a couple and the death of their parents.

Also, the belief that pre-industrial families were large in size needs correction. Generalizing from the large families in the underdeveloped nations today, many observers have concluded that this must have been the case for pre-industrial families in Europe and the United States. Although very large families with eight to twelve children were not uncommon, they were by no means the norm. Because, for one thing, people married later than they do today and, for another, women experienced menopause at an earlier age, the years for married couples to have children were fewer. Also, the family size was limited by the likely occurrence of premature death by one of the spouses. Perhaps most importantly, death regularly struck all age categories. Those living in towns were particularly vulnerable because of a lack of sanitation and impurities in the water supply. In fact, people living in towns did not reproduce their own population size and instead depended on migration from rural areas to maintain their numbers. On the average, around a third of the infants died during their first year, and in some areas half of the children died before the age of ten. Young adults had a comparatively high mortality rate as well. As a result, family size among the peasantry averaged two or three children at any one point in time, although the number of children born was quite a bit higher (Giddens, 1982: 134-35). Also, family sizes were not dramatically larger during the early part of this century. Around 1900 the average family included only four children, despite the reduction in infant deaths. By 1930 this was reduced to three children, and today the rounded average is two children.

Even more relevant to the question of a "golden age" of the family, it is now recognized that in pre-industrial societies marriage was not the focal point of emotional attachment or dependence at any level in the class system. Relations between spouses as well as between parents and children were not especially affectionate or intimate. According to Lawrence Stone, "Conventional wisdom was that happiness could only be anticipated in the next world, not in this, and sex was not a pleasure but a sinful necessity justified only by the need to propagate the race." Stone continues, "The expectation of life was so low that it was imprudent to become too emotionally dependent upon any other human being"(Stone, 1977:5). Although Stone may be overstating his case, his study produced massive evidence that relationships among family members were marked by a relative absence of emotional content. Marriage was not a matter about which an individual could be that selective anyway. For peasants and artisans, marriage was usually an economic necessity. For the property-owning class and the royalty, marriage was a collective decision by family and kin who used marital ties as a means of securing the inheritance of property or of maximizing economic advantages or forming political alliances. In both cases, marital bonds were practical matters, too important to be left to the emotional whims of the individuals involved. Notions of romantic love did flourish, but only in courtly circles, and even there romance was *not* associated with marriage and families.

How much expectations of the family have changed since that time can be appreciated if we recognize how inappropriate the *Papal Exhortation on the Family* would have been two or three hundred years ago. Identifying the family as the domestic church, a community where one can attain spiritual growth, would have been scarcely comprehensible in societies where there was a strict division between the family and the church. During the several hundred years prior to the Industrial Revolution, the church was a separate institution where one sought guidance and salvation, whereas the family was an economic necessity with little pretense as to enhancing the spiritual, intellectual, or psychological growth of its members. In contrast, contemporary patterns of intimate relations seem far better suited to facilitate satisfaction, fulfillment, and growth of its members in many areas. Despite the negative remarks that predominate in the papal discussion of a number of specific contemporary situations, the exhortation does seem to recognize this potential within family patterns. Otherwise, the document would have read quite differently, with much less flexibility for individual family and pastor discretion.

Those who speak of a family crisis and the decay resulting from the dissolution of marriages or the changes in sexual behavior frequently lack an adequate historical perspective. The dissolution of marriages during previous centuries both in Europe and the United States was quite common, although it occurred most often as a result of the premature death of a spouse rather than through divorce. Divorce was expensive and much more difficult to obtain, and thus an option only available to the wealthy. For example, in Britain before 1857, a private act of Parliament was required to obtain a divorce, something only the most wealthy could afford (Haralambos, 1980: 364). Instead of divorce, desertion by one spouse was much more common. Some analysts have argued that the proportion of children affected by "broken marriages" was at least as high in the past as it is today. In addition, in some European countries during recent history, the rates of "illegitimate" births were as great or greater than they are today. Pre-marital sexual intercourse was usual for both sexes and was not regarded as a hindrance to subsequent marriages. But all of this does not mean that the family has not changed. Western societies have been experiencing profound changes in marital patterns that are largely the culmination of centuries of economic changes. The fact that these shifts in family patterns appear to be especially concentrated within the past fifteen years does not mean that the structural basis for them had not been established long before. In fact recent changes are simply a speed up of trends that have continued at least throughout this century, and they do not represent a dramatic reversal or a qualitatively new situation.

THE FAMILY AND THE INDUSTRIAL REVOLUTION

Many contemporary changes in family patterns can be traced to the effects of the Industrial Revolution. The period of the Industrial Revolution in the United States spanned the years from approximately 1840 to 1920. Before discussing these changes, I wish to emphasize that they are not the result of an economic determinism, whereby economic changes caused, in the strict sense, alterations in family forms. In fact, recent historical research has demonstrated that some changes that previously were attributed to industrialism actually occurred *before* the beginning of the Industrial Revolution. For example, during the eighteenth century, or prior to industrialism for most Western societies, nuclear families developed an identity that more clearly separated them from their kinship group. As a consequence, the emotional bonds between spouses and between parents and children intensified (Skolnick, 1983: 117; Stone, 1979: 22). Carl N. Degler traces this shift in the United States roughly between the years 1780 and 1830 (Degler, 1980: pp. 9-25). Nevertheless, it does appear that changes in family patterns are closely intertwined with changes that accompanied the Industrial Revolution and the development of capitalism in Western societies, even if we cannot always sort out the direction of causality. The overall pattern is clear: in industrialized societies previous family forms have given way to others that are better suited to contemporary conditions of social and economic life.

One profound change is that the economic productive functions of the family have drastically declined. Families are simply not the locus of material production as they were when most people lived as peasants, farmers, and independent artisans. Also, home-handicraft manufacturing declined. Although this point hardly needs elaboration, it is important to recognize that a shift of production out of the confines of family networks and into centers of manufacturing and industry created markets for the labor that had been deprived of its independent means of sustenance. The unequal relations to the labor markets experienced by different classes, sexes, nationalities, ethnicities, and residents of different geographical locations are the basis of much of the social inequality in capitalist societies today. This economic and occupational transition also completely undermined the primary basis around which pre-industrial families were composed. Family members were incorporated separately into labor markets. The culmination was the separation of the home from the workshop.

It is generally recognized by scholars that an urban, industrial environment strengthens the nuclear family with respect to the traditional kinship networks. Even though living arrangements were more nuclear than extended in pre-industrial Europe and the United States, kinship relations were a far more important determinant of social status, the well-being and security of one's immediate family, and the fate of individuals than is the case today. One major reason for their decline is that kin relations are no longer needed to contribute to the family's economic productive function. Also, the increase in geographical mobility that has accompanied industrialism has made it impossible for many relatives to participate in the daily lives of those outside the nuclear family.

Accompanying the passage of the means of the subsistence from individual families to owners of capital, was a reduction in family size. Under the conditions of wage labor, children became an economic liability rather than an asset. This reduction in family size has had a particularly important impact on the lives of women. Since the death rates of infants and children have declined dramatically and life expectancy has risen, women now spend a much smaller proportion of their life in pregnancy and care of small children. As the papers of Dana Hiller and Thomas Harblin document, this has been coupled with an upward trend in the proportion of women employed outside the home during this century. The rise has been especially pronounced within the past twenty years, particularly within the category of married women with offspring living at home. Even during the fifteen years immediately following World War II when the ideology glorifying female domestication was at its height, more women than ever joined the work force. This occurred during the period when married employed women were looked upon as deviants, so much so that *Life* magazine in 1956 denounced the "disease" of working women (Skolnick, 1983: 27). In fact, before World War II, most employed wives were found in the lower classes. By 1960, women from all classes were in the labor force or were looking for jobs. This, in effect, answered the question of whether women should be employed outside the household. While the employment rate for women was rising, married women with children were made to feel guilty: their alleged neglect of their families was thought to have a detrimental effect on their children. A recent review of the literature on this subject found, in contrast, a remarkable consensus among researchers that a mother's employment is not a crucial variable in a child's well-being and development (Skolnick, 1983: 28-29).

TOWARD A COMPANIONATE AFFECTIVE FAMILY

One important consequence of the structural changes has been that the roles, duties, obligations, and privileges of husbands and wives, males and females, are becoming increasingly similar. The strict segregation of activities by sex which was rigid in pre-industrial societies is now substantially diminished. Men and women, whether married or single, whether with children or not, now engage in similar kinds of activities. Not only do women contribute in increasing numbers to the family's income, but men have slowly begun to take up household tasks that used to be regarded as women's work (although men's contributions often are more symbolic than comprehensive in this area). Patricia Voydanoff in her paper refers to this as a shift toward a "symmetrical family" where there is "a greater overlap [between male and female activities and duties] and decreased differentiation according to traditional sex role norms."

Another consequence is that the criteria of marriage have gradually shifted over the past several hundred years from more practical economic concerns to those based on affection (love) and companionship. Lawrence Stone identifies this shift as established in portions of the middle and upper sectors of English society by 1750, although this pattern spread to encompass the aristocracy, artisans, and wage earners much later—only by the end of the nineteenth century (Stone, 1979: 22). More recently, expectations for meeting these criteria have risen. Presently, couples are supposed to share similar interests, hold compatible values and goals, be close companions, communicate freely and honestly, have a mutually satisfying sexual relationship, and facilitate each other's personal growth. The paper by Stanley Saxton and Michael Katovich develops several dimensions and supporting conditions of such a relationship. However, heightened expectations for intimate relationships can become unrealistic and paradoxically doom some marriages to dissatisfaction. But, there is little indication that people are backing off from their expectations.

We can call this kind of union a "companionate affective" marriage or family. While it has been compatible for the previous 150 years with traditional sex role separation, with the employed male taking on the instrumental role and the domestic female fulfilling the expressive role, this kind of marriage has been moving toward an egalitarian base, with more equal contributions by both spouses to child-rearing duties, household tasks, major family decisions, and family income.

There seems to be recognition of this marital basis in the papal exhortation:

> The situation in which the family finds itself presents positive and negative aspects...On the one hand, in fact, there is a more lively awareness of personal freedom and greater attention to the quality of interpersonal relationships in marriage, in promoting the dignity of women, to responsible procreation, to the education of children. There is also an awareness of the need for the development of interfamily relationships, for reciprocal spiritual and material assistance, the rediscovery of the ecclesial mission proper to the family and its responsibility for the building of a more just society (FC§6).

The exhortation appears to hold high spiritual expectations for contemporary families, ones that would be inappropriate for marriages not based on criteria such as close companionship and shared interests. The document further indicates disapproval with certain forms of inequality both within a family and in the societal positions of women:

> ...one cannot but observe that in the specific area of family life a widespread social and cultural tradition has considered women's role to be

exclusively that of wife and mother, without adequate access to public functions, which have generally been reserved for men (FC§23).

The pope also refers critically to sexual discrimination in education, employment, and wages, and to the harmful effects of attitudes of a "wrong superiority of male prerogatives which humiliates women and inhibits the development of healthy family relationships" (FC§25).

Two complementary changes, at least in American society, have corresponded to the emergence of companionate affective marriages built on an egalitarian base: a shift toward introspection and a rise in the education level. Compared to twenty-five years ago, Americans are far more likely to speak about themselves, their difficulties, and their satisfactions in psychological terms. Further, more people are willing to admit to having problems in their marriages, with their children, and in their jobs. Also, they are less likely to define themselves exclusively in terms of their social roles and statuses. Instead, people are more likely to mention inner feelings and experiences and personal qualities as keys to their "true selves." In general, there has been an increase in sensitivity to the quality of interpersonal relationships, both within the family and at work (Skolnick, 1983: 38-39). I would like to suggest that this shift goes along with contemporary expectations for marriage. It is no longer acceptable for "breadwinning" or housekeeping abilities to be the primary criteria of a good husband and father or wife and mother. Instead, criteria that may be enhanced by introspective qualities, such as close companionship and deep communication are increasingly regarded as essential. This has also had ramifications for childrearing practices. Parental attention has shifted from concern that children were healthy and obedient to preoccupation with their psychological motives and potentials. Child behavior, like that of adults, is more likely to be viewed in terms of "needs" and "stages."

Also, there is a correspondence between educational attainment and communication skills. With the rise in the educational level, it would appear that an increasing proportion of people are more adept at interpersonal communication. Education also seems to make people more introspective and more critical, both of themselves and of prevailing ideas and institutions. While this may lead to heightened dissatisfaction with intimate relationships, these are also qualities associated with marital expectations.

MARITAL BREAKDOWN

At first glance, the proposition that Western cultures are moving toward companionate affective marriages with an egalitarian base does not seem to be compatible with the increase in marital dissolution. The rise in divorce rates is not unique to the United States. Many countries that traditionally have had comparatively low divorce rates, such as Great Britain, France, Belgium, and Japan, have experienced proportional increases in divorce rates that are roughly equivalent to, or exceed, that experienced by the United States during the past twenty-five years. If the basically upbeat picture of contemporary intimate relationships that has been presented in this paper so far is accurate, then why is it that an increasing proportion of couples are choosing to terminate their marriages?

First, statistics that chronicle the rise in divorce rates and arguments that connect those to an increase in marital breakdown need to be qualified. We have already pointed out that in the past desertion by one spouse was frequently taken as a means to end a union. As divorce has become easier to obtain and the stigma that previously surrounded it has dissipated, then divorce, or legal separation, has become regarded as the most honorable way to terminate an unsatisfactory marriage. We simply do not know what divorce rates would have been in previous decades and centuries if divorce had been more affordable and obtainable, but they certainly would have been considerably higher. Also, records of divorce in the past were less reliable, most likely in the direction of underrecording the actual number of divorces as well as desertions and separations. In addition, some of the marriages which are ended by divorce today would have been ended by the death of one of the spouses in the past. Divorce and separation become far more acceptable options when there is little chance of the death of one's unsatisfactory spouse within a decade or two.

When examined over a longer time span, the apparent rapid increase in divorce rates over the past fifteen years does not seem so dramatic. Divorce rates have been rising since at least the middle of the nineteenth century. In fact, if on a graph one were to record for every year of the past century the proportion of all marriages that ended in divorce and then were to draw a line that best fit the data, one would find a smooth upward curve indicating a gradually rising divorce rate. There are several variations from this trend: a higher-than-expected divorce rate among those who married during the period from the late 1920s to the early 1940s (corresponding to the Depression) and among those who married in the late 1960s and early 1970s (the data stops with 1973), as well as a lower-than-expected divorce rate among those who married in the decade after World War II (Skolnick, 1983: 44-47).

On the basis of this and other longitudinal data, it now appears that marriage, divorce, and fertility patterns during the late 1940s and 1950s represent an exception to long-term trends. We do not often hear the 1950s referred to as a deviant period, but during the fifteen years after World War II people began to marry more frequently, have more children, and divorce less often, all of which represents a clear reversal of historical patterns. The present high divorce rates coupled with fewer marriages and a decline in fertility may differ from figures for the previous generation, but they are consistent with long-term trends. One study has commented that, "Had the 1940s and 1950s not happened, today's young adults would appear to be behaving normally"(Masnick and Bane, 1980: 2).

Social science has been moving toward an explanation of the rise in divorces as well as the growth in alternatives to marriages, such as cohabitation, trial marriages, single parent families, and gay relationships. Rather than interpret these as representing a decline in marriage and the family, something to be either deplored or celebrated, an increasing proportion of scholars and researchers now argue that contemporary patterns represent a triumph of what we have called a companionate affective form of marriage and the family. Accordingly, the increase in divorces may not indicate a decline in the family as an institution or deep dissatisfaction with marriage, but rather represents a growing determination to make marriages and other forms of intimate relationships rewarding and satisfying (see for example, Fletcher, 1966; Levitan and Belous, 1981; Bane, 1976). Also, a high divorce rate has been coupled with a high rate of remarriage: 75 percent of those divorced will remarry within five years. In addition, most marriages are long-term; few people marry more than twice.

It is clear that expectations of marriage have not only changed but also have been rising. Spouses now hold out higher standards for their marriages than they did in the past. Also, the norms have changed regarding unsatisfactory relationships. It is no longer judged admirable for a person to endure a dismal relationship that has little hope of improvement. Historical evidence indicates that "empty shell" marriages, where marriage exists in name only, are more likely to end in divorce and separation than in the past (Haralambos, 1980: 362). The reasons that were given in the past for remaining in an unsatisfactory relationship, such as for the good of the children or to save embarrassment or to maintain status in the community, are no longer regarded as legitimate. Although divorce is certainly not idealized, it is no longer regarded as a sign of moral flaw or of deep personal failure. Rather it has become an event, usually traumatic, that many people recognize the odds of encountering.

MARITAL SATISFACTION

Rising marital expectations and increases in divorce do not seem to have had a negative impact on marital satisfaction. Despite increased attention by the media, social workers, marriage counselors, psychologists, and clerics to the problems of contemporary marriages, most studies reveal a continuing personal commitment to marriage and family life. Couples may be more willing than in the past to admit to problems in their marriages and families, and perhaps some issues that were not considered important before have now become a source of tension and conflict. But this is combined with a dedication to discuss problems openly and an attempt to work them out. Both Patricia Voydanoff and Dana Hiller in their papers suggest on the basis of limited data that marital satisfaction appears to be positively related to characteristics associated with egalitarian marriages and families.

One method of analyzing changes in the ways people regard their marriages is to compare how men and women characterized their relationships in the past with how they do so today. During the mid-1920s and again during the mid-1930s, Robert and Helen Lynd (1929) selected Muncie, Indiana, as the site for their research on a typical small American city. Patterns in Middletown, the authors' pseudonym for Muncie, were interpreted as representing mainstream American life. Employing a variety of research techniques, the Lynds examined, among other things, occupations, schools, child rearing, social inequalities, religious practices, community values, and marriages. In reviewing marriage patterns in Middletown during the 1920s, several notable points emerge. Romantic love was regarded "as the only valid basis for marriage," and divorces were increasingly granted on the basis of a mutual lack of affection between spouses. Divorces were becoming commonplace and easier to obtain. The Lynds quoted Dorothy Dix, an elderly woman whose syndicated advice column appeared in Middletown's leading newspaper, as expressing a sentiment with which they felt most Middletown residents would agree:

> The reason there are more divorces is that people are demanding more of life than they used to... In former times... they expected to settle down to a life of hard work... and just putting up with each other... A divorced woman was a disgraced woman.... But now we view the matter differently. We see that no good purpose is achieved by keeping two people together who have come to hate each other (128).

The Lynds also found Middletown to be in the midst of a sexual revolution, spurred by changing norms and the impact of automobiles and movie theaters. Women's clothes were designed to emphasize sex, and sex was a dominate theme in popular literature and the movies. A wide gulf, or generation gap, separated the attitudes and behavior of Middletown's parents and their adolescent offspring. Even the Lynds worried about the future of the American family.

Despite the contemporary quality of these observations, the Lynds also discovered that "a high degree of companionship is not regarded as essential for marriage." More strikingly, husband and wife typically did not share much in the way of mutual interests. The orbits of men and women in their daily tasks and leisure activities were quite separate. The Lynds did write that "There are some homes in Middletown among both working and business class families which one cannot enter without being aware of a constant undercurrent of sheer delight, of fresh, spontaneous interest between husband and wife." "But," the Lynds continue, "such homes stand out by reason of their relative rarity" (130).

More typical of Middletown's families during the 1920s were ones where the absence of shared interests, lack of communication, and sharp division of sex roles created tension, hostility, and resentment between husbands and wives.

> The husband must "support" his family, but... recurrent "hard times" make support of their families periodically impossible for many workers; the wife must make a home for her husband and care for her children, but she is increasingly spending her days in gainful employment outside the home; husband and wife must cleave to each other in the sex relation, but fear of pregnancy frequently makes this relation a dread for one or both of them; affection between the two is regarded as the basis of marriage, but sometimes in the day-to-day struggle this seems to be a memory rather than a present help... More than one wife seems to think of her husband less as an individual rather than as a focus of problems and fears—anxiety about loss of job, dissappoint- ment over failure in promotion, fear of conception—the center of a whole complex of things to be avoided. To many husbands their wives have become associated with weariness, too many children, and other people's washings (129).

Significantly, not one of the sixty-eight working class wives who were interviewed mentioned her husband when asked what things gave her "courage to go on when thoroughly discouraged" (129).

Between 1976 and 1978, a team of researchers headed by Theodore Caplow of the University of Virginia returned to Muncie to survey the changes that had taken place during the preceding fifty years. Their first published volume was specifically concerned with family patterns. Al- though their study has been criticized for emphasizing family rituals and harmony, thus overlooking tensions and conflicts within families, their findings still serve as an instructive base of comparison with the Lynds conclusions. The recent study found widespread concern in Middletown over the future of the American family and the general feeling that our era was experiencing a crisis of family life. Residents expressed serious reservations over the rising divorce rate (Middletown's divorce rate was in line with the national average), thought that divorces were "too easy" to obtain, and deplored divorce in the abstract. However, the results of the Caplow (1982) study indicated that there had been an increase in family solidarity within the past fifty years. Also, spousal communication was now more open and covered a wider range of topics. The kind of depressing, noncommunicative marriage the Lynds described as typical during the 1920s was now a rarity. There was less of a separation between men and women by traditional sex roles, although the division of labor between spouses was still prominent. Subjects that were rarely discussed between spouses fifty years ago, such as birth control and family finances, were no longer considered inappropriate. Younger married couples seemed to be the most open and competent communicators. The rise in divorce rates was probably one of the main reasons why contemporary marriages in Middletown seem so satisfactory when compared to those in the past; today most unhappy marriages break up. And, although the researchers found a "generation gap" between adolescents and parents that the parents thought was getting wider, their findings showed that the "gap" was less than during previous generations and that parents and children were now spending *more* time together than previously.

Recent public attention to serious family problems and brutalities, such as husband-wife violence, child-beating and child neglect, incest, and psychological abuse, must be understood within the context of changing norms and rising expectations. These topics were previously ignored, and such behavior was associated with what was thought to be only a pathological fringe. The "discovery" that these are widespread problems does not mean that they did not exist before, only that they were not publicly discussed. We do not even know if incidence of such behavior has actually risen, although public awareness of them and related topics, such as rape, certainly has (Skolnick, 1983: 16). It is plausible that there has been an increase in family violence, since as expectations are raised and companionship and emotional satisfaction are emphasized, frustrations may result from failures to realize an ideal in practice. However, we need to recognize that what previously may have been seen as harsh, but acceptable, ways of treating women and disciplining children are now more likely to be defined as unacceptable (and illegal) abuse, although serious and sometimes life-threatening family violence is still too often tolerated by police, social service agencies, and the courts.

There are several substantial barriers to achieving egalitarian families in practice. First, as Linda Majka has pointed out in her paper, gender inequalities are institutionalized in the occupational structure through its separate labor markets. Employment opportunities for women are still predominantly underpaid and in sex-typed or sex-segregated occupations. These are powerful forces that keep many women (as well as minority populations) in unfulfilling, low-paying, and insecure employment. After summarizing several important recent studies on female employment, Degler concludes that most women's employment remains tied to the needs of their families (Degler, 1980: 449-53). "Women's work in the main is still shaped around the family, while the family is still shaped around the work of men..."(p. 436). "Women are still the primary child-rearers, even when they work, and the purpose of their work...is to support and advance the family, not to realize themselves as individuals" (p. 453). As a result, the widespread entry of women into the labor force has not resulted in equiv-alent wages for both men and women. Also, the economic recessions of the 1970s and early 1980s have worked against family security and have contributed to the "feminization of poverty."

In addition, equivalent division of household tasks between spouses is far from reality in most families. Men now cook, clean, shop, and tend to infants, but usually *only* when it is convenient for them to do so (Davidson and Gordon, 1979: 42-43; Degler, 1980: 465-67). These two patterns of women receiving less income and having more domestic responsibilities reenforce each other. The worlds of jobs/careers and families are closely tied together.

IMPLICATIONS AND CONCLUSIONS

The perspective on the family that has been presented in this paper views changes occurring in family life as offering opportunities rather than representing a decline or breakdown. Egalitarian relationships based on companionship and affection are well suited to facilitate personal fulfill-ment and promote intellectual, emotional, and spiritual development. The papal exhortation appears to recognize this opportunity; otherwise, there would not have been such a strong emphasis on the family as a "domestic church" and as a "communion of persons."

However, there also appears to be a wide range of patterns associated with companionate affective families that the pope continues to view as harmful and contrary to church teachings. These include comparatively high rates of divorce and remarriage, cohabitation, trial marriages, and the widespread use of contraceptives. I would like to suggest that these are not aberrations from changing patterns of intimate relationships but rather represent intrinsic components of such change. This does not mean that the institution of the family is eroding, but rather that it includes a broader range of alternatives than before, all of which may be as well, if not better, suited for personal fulfillment and growth, depending on the individuals involved.

Michael Place's paper captures the theological dimensions of this dilemma. The shifts from classical to an historicist perspective in theological methodology, from an objective morality to recognition of the conflictual nature of moral values, and from the church as an authoritative director of a person's faith to ascribing greater competency to the lay individual are all expressed in abstract terms in the exhortation. However, when the document addresses specifics, such as the purpose and indissolubility of marriage and significance of human sexuality, the papal prescriptions return to the traditional guidelines that exhibit little recognition of contemporary developments in theology. Along with clarifying contemporary changes in family life, I hope my own contribution to this volume makes it clear that recent shifts in theology are far more appropriate for facilitating personal development and growth within the context of contemporary forms of intimate relationships.

REFERENCES

Bane, Mary Jo, 1976. *Here To Stay*. New York: Basic Books.

Caplow, Theodore and H. M. Bahr, B. A. Chadwick, R. Hill, and M. H. Willemson. 1982. *Middletown Families: Fifty Years of Change and Continuity*. Minneapolis: University of Minnesota Press.

Davidson, Laurie and Laura Kramer Gordon. 1979. *The Sociology of Gender*. Chicago: Rand McNally.

Degler, Carl N. 1980. *At Odds: Women and the Family in America from the Revolution to the Present*. New York: Oxford University Press.

Donzelot, Jacques. 1979. *The Policing of Families*. New York: Pantheon Books.

Fletcher, Ronald. 1966. *The Family and Marriage in Britain*. Harmondsworth, England: Penguin Books.

Foucault, Michel. 1981. *The History of Sexuality*. New York: Vintage Books.

Giddens, Anthony. 1982. *Sociology: A Brief but Critical Introduction*. New York: Harcourt Brace Jovanovich, Inc.

Haralambos, Michael. 1980. *Sociology: Themes and Perspectives*. Slough, England: University Tutorial Press Limited.

Lasch, Christopher. 1977. *Haven in a Heartless World: The Family Besieged*. New York: Basic Books.

Laslett, Peter. 1972. "Mean Household Size in England since the Sixteenth Century,"in Peter Laslett, ed., *Household and Family in Past Time*. Cambridge, England: Cambridge University Press.

Levitan, S. A. and R. S. Belous. 1981. *What's Happening to the American Family?* Baltimore: John Hopkins Press.

Lynd, Robert S. and Helen Merrell Lynd. 1929. Reprinted 1956. *Middletown: A Study in Modern American Culture*. New York: Harcourt, Brace and World, Inc.

Masnick, G. and M. J. Bane. 1980. *The Nation's Families: 1960-1990*. Boston: Auburn House.

Pope John Paul II. 1982. *On The Family/Familiaris Consortio*. Washington, D.C.: United States Catholic Conference.

Skolnick, Arlene S. 1983. *The Intimate Environment: Exploring Marriage and the Family*, Third Edition. Boston: Little, Brown and Company.

Stone, Lawrence. 1977. Reprinted 1979. *The Family, Sex and Marriage in England 1500-1800*. London: Weidenfeld and Nicolson. New York: Harper and Row.

13

Familiaris Consortio

A Pastoral View

Rev. Leonard G. Urban

FREDERICK, COLORADO

I am writing from the heart. No guise or subterfuge here. The matter is too serious for fictional drama or exaggeration for the sake of shock. Truth comes so often in stark reality that it would be irreverent to dissemble.

Not long ago, earlier today, in fact, I spent an hour with a woman I've known for eight years. Her life, to my assessment, had been simple, at least comparatively so for our times. She came to informally express, if that's the word, that after eighteen years of marriage she was leaving her husband. Reason? Her husband's infidelity, of which she had been totally unaware until then. If such things are ever simple, the story was simply this: over a period of years he had been coming home increasingly late. Alleged reason? Work at the office; a change of position in the company requiring more time and more energy. The ember of suspicion smoldered eventually into conflagration and she confronted him, "Are you really working this late? Or is there something you should tell me?" Answer: "Yes, there is. I have been seeing someone, how do you say it? having a relationship with her for four years."

There are, of course, the effects that never quite run their course. There is the guilt and recrimination for what was left undone, unsaid, which might have redirected their marriage toward glorious success, the kind too blithely touted in journals and life-style magazines. What happens in the soul looks cold and analytic on paper; another statistic, a case study of the ongoing travail which visits its injury on the lives of the unfortunate, for reasons inexplicable.

What remains is a plethora of mixed memories, spoiled now by a too swift revelation of human weakness, perhaps a touch of malice, or the mysterious blending of both. There are the hollow, suffering eyes of uncomprehending children; there is a disillusioned spouse, a broken family. They are familiar consorts, these fractured people; for them there is no community in the unity of purpose.

Singularly noteworthy is the fact that such an incident is not isolated. It happens in the lives of many, knows no barriers, excludes no class for the sake of dignity. Today the broken family takes up permanent residence and leaves hardly any individual unaffected.

FAMILIARIS CONSORTIO

It is no wonder that the pope and his experts are writing letters, appealing to what is better in human kind, hoping to help us find that self which the psychologist contends is worthy of our search. We are reminded that the search best begins in the family with its social role, its expression of value, its base for political and community direction (FC§44).

The question within the question of *Familiaris Consortio* simply asks in what way Christian family life may be discovered to resemble what has been given us in the message of the gospel. What is a Christian family? Are there specific ingredients that distinguish Christian family life from the current pervading attitude that seems to advocate self-direction and studied indifference? Does the theologian have something to add, a dimension somehow unheeded or acknowledged only superficially and in part? *Familiaris Consortio* thinks so and offers a "way of life" based on the rich exhortation of Jesus to follow a path to which we are called by virtue of our baptism. Only by the acceptance of the gospels can we expect the hopes we place in marriage to be fulfilled (FC§3).

The Promethean effort exerted by Christians of all ages has been characterized by a delving into the meaning of the "Good News." What can be found there which is pertinent, appropriate to our lives, transcends lesser values, and is universal? Exactly what is the message of Jesus and more specifically, how does it apply to family life, which might turn out to be the only life we have? Who does not belong to a family, a group of persons whose objective is to gather in co-operation with others toward the attainment of hopeful goals?

Jesus came transforming thoughts and attitudes that were deeply entrenched in the minds of people. He was a paradox, a surprise to the molded and settled thinking of complacent tradition. Jesus is a new person, not meant to slip comfortably into the custom and prevailing values of the day. He speaks in terms of contradiction, offering a way of life that finds gain in loss, the first place by being last, and giving away freely what one has. He advocates simplicity over clutter, peace over violence, even at the cost of life, purity of intention, and a willing hand held out to those who suffer the capricious setbacks of life. He advocates the ready relinquishment of personal good for the sake of justice and looks upon persecution as a way of life. He speaks as God's word and suggests that we are whole when we clothe, feed, and minister in every possible way to those who are in need.

The message of Jesus is clear and clearly applies to Christians, whatever their setting.

MARRIAGE AND FAMILY LIFE

What about marriage and the family then? The prime seat of life is contained here. Whatever we have seen and experienced has had its beginning and growth in that setting. It is in the context of the family that we come to know the Christian message, that we develop an awareness of what Jesus proposes and recommends as a fuller and more satisfactory life-style. *Familiaris Consortio* suggests that God makes the fullest revelation today through marriage and family life: "The parents not only communicate the Gospel to their children, but from their children they can themselves receive the same Gospel as deeply lived by them" (FC§52).

Perhaps family life needs, more than any other reality, a sense of the gospel. If this is asking much, it is candidly because much can be expected. Over against so many values which are self-oriented and promise personal returns, the gospel pleads for a consideration of others. The implementation of such a principle speaks to serving one's spouse, caring for the deeper needs of children, and a willingness to grow continually in tolerance and forgiveness.

That sort of affective response cannot be learned in a day, or brought out without profound commitment. Such tasks are obviously the result of a faith response which is integrated with life itself. To think of others, to really love them, to want their continual welfare, demands an intimate attachment of our lives to the gospel, not only to bits and pieces, but to all of it from its beginning to its end.

Is there a distinguishing character which is clearly visible in the Christian family? If the criterion offered by Jesus has to do with love at cost and personal effort, then those realities ought to be readily apparent in families that reflect the gospel message. The assurance of Jesus that passing observers would know his disciples by the love they showed to one another should be nowhere more apparent than in the Christian family. In practical terms this means that Christian family members should strive to be in our time what Jesus was in his, a person for others, a person of all seasons. To speak of family only in terms of upward mobility, moving ahead, living life to the fullest, misses the essence of the message which Jesus teaches of dying to find life and of taking the last place to be first. The truly Christian family must seek to be defined in other terms, terms which involve the meaning of Christian marriage as a commitment to a different path.

In a more refined understanding of the meaning of our lives, we have striven for a liberty that has freed us from old restraints where religious expression is concerned. We have come to a newer and more comfortable approach to God as a good and gracious parent rather than a taskmaster and sovereign lord. We have justifiably asked for less authority from the institution, fewer laws, and more meaning in seeking the good of the members of the church. Such developments have been welcome and bring their own sense of relief, a late but pleasant respite from enervating guilt and fruitless accusations. Many of us have become more comfortable and relaxed where religion and faith are concerned. Every effort to be free of former restraints has its subtle effect. Freedom might imperceptibly come to mean irresponsibility, a kind of intangible permission that where formerly too much was demanded, now nothing may be asked.

The de-emphasis of structure and authoritarianism have concomitantly brought about their own effects. While wishing to begin a new era, we have at times neglected lasting and substantial elements in what we now call the old Church. If the Christian family is to fulfill its prophetic role by welcoming and announcing the word of God, it must do so as an expression of the central element in its own life (FC§51). *Familiaris Consortio* offers a variety of suggestions on how this can be accomplished.

To begin with, family life must not be begun without preparation and anticipation (FC§66). We deem it foolish to undertake careers, maintain professions, even keep up with the daily business of coping with life, without adequate preparation. We organize, calculate, and analyze. It is unthinkable that we should be caught short, hands empty at the back of the parade. We pride ourselves on being current and we use a dozen aphorisms to assure ourselves that we are aware, with it, and not left behind holding the bag.

Too many love-swept couples look upon marriage, the family, and the learning of meaningful values as automatic, somehow having their magical effect if we give God his due by "marrying in the Church." Some couples resent the interference of classes, interviews, and genuine solicitude by interested persons who want to help them enrich their lives. After all, isn't love a powerful force that surmounts all obstacles? Sometimes preparation classes and seminars lack professional impact because we ministers are just beginning and not at all used to our roles in a new Church. But the message remains concrete: there is a universal hope held by everyone that marriage and family life will become better instead of worse. But such wonderful phenomena are not realized by love or resolution or money or long talks after midnight. These may help, but there is no substitute for adequate preparation.

For established families with children, catechesis, that is, teaching the message of the gospel, is essential (FC§39). Traditionally, education has been consigned to the institution, to schools and classrooms. Parents have not felt themselves qualified to speak to their children about God, to read and discuss the Scripture, to speak honestly to them about Jesus and what kinds of response his message should evoke. There is a subtle fear in many family settings that failure lurks behind conscious efforts to teach, to give compelling example, and to offer assistance. Parents are often too ready to give *things* rather than *themselves*; they amass goods rather than cultivate quality relationships. Fertile opportunities for acquiring deeper human qualities such as justice and political awareness, compassion for the poor, and care for certain minority people, are often overlooked or excused because people do not want to trouble their children and dislocate a comfortable family life. Too often the opposite is true, and the turning in toward self is frought with discontent and restless confusion.

Forty years ago families gathered to say the Rosary, the Litany of the Saints, or other prayers. Candle lighting in homes carried the notion of leaving one's presence with God. Ceremonies of enthronement and blessings of homes gave confidence, peace, and a sense of protection in the house. Such rituals gave families an attitude of belonging, an identity and continuity with Church tradition. It is not important for us to retrieve and maintain the precise forms of prayer and ritual in family life. It is very important for us to create something to take their place (FC§59). Is there a time for prayer in the family? (FC§60). Do the sacraments offer an opportunity for expressing what is significant in family life? If confession and Eucharist have become dull and uninteresting, could it be that we do not understand their meaning? (FC§57). When we hear of children refusing to go to church, announcing their disinterest and boredom, is it not already too late, because tradition, ritual, and ceremony have been virtually absent from their lives?

POLITICAL ACTION

Jesus was a person who went about doing good. He defined a neighbor as any person who might have fallen among robbers on the side of the road and was waiting for assistance. He befriended the forgotten and neglected people in society: prostitutes, tax collectors, and erstwhile Pharisees who came in the middle of the night to speak to him. People asked outlandish and ridiculous favors of him because they knew he was a "soft touch" and of easy persuasion. He offered new hope in forgiveness to prodigal fathers and to foolish shepherds who would leave everything for the sake of something smaller and apparently negligible. In a word, Jesus served the needs of others. He revealed who God was and what He had to say to all of us.

In the end, Jesus told us to go and do likewise, to be persons of service, to care for the needs of others, to remember the forgotten, to bring new hope where before there was only futility.

If God can be found in the Christian family, it surely must be in its service to the needs of others. Somehow in family life we are all called to those same realities which were revealed in Jesus. This not-so-simple message calls for personal realization in parents who recognize the needs of "the hungry, poor, the old, the sick, drug victims and those who have no family" (FC§47). There are no options here, no choice of what to do. This is a clear expression of the family's call to service (FC§48). Children and family members have a right to exercise their gifts for the good of others. Mothers and fathers communicate who Jesus was by how they live out their own roles as Christians. Families must preserve what is best in society by fostering a sensitivity for the worth of every individual. Such ideals cannot be realized where there are rifts and hatreds in communities, rejection of certain persons on the basis of stereotypes, and long-standing prejudice.

COMMUNITY SERVICE

The family is not an isolated unit. Obviously the health of any individual contributes to the health of the community (FC§42). The community is composed of many members, each with something to offer; it is a whole only by reason of its gathered parts. The age of rugged individualism, existance apart from the total community, is past, or it should be.

The Christian family functions in association with, and dependence upon, other families. (FC§43) All families together constitute a direction and a force by which Christian attitudes and values are witnessed. Political and social directions are directly influenced by the health of the family. This means that family members must interest themselves in movements and in the signs of the times, they must know what is happening and be willing to participate in what shapes and gives form to social and political response. (FC§48)

This transformation of vision, from living one's life in privacy and disinterest to sharing one's thoughts and gifts with the community, is critical for the vitality of any parish or congregation. Evangelization has come to mean preaching, even haranguing, about God. The idea carries with it a notion of persuasion and the need to act for the sake of a God who waits impatiently. But true evangelization has much more to do with bearing witness and being of service to others. When something has merit, it doesn't have to be forced and pushed forward as though life couldn't be lived without it. The most valuable kind of evangelization has a gentler approach. It may be strongly enunciated, but it leaves the final decision of acceptance up to the hearer. (FC§52)

SUPPORTING THE FAMILY

If we have neglected to provide adequate preparation for entering marriage, being aware of what that commitment entails, we have been equally negligent of the need to nurture marriages after they take place. Sadly, many married couples who endure a variety of tensions do not seek professional assistance or support from other members of the community. Many couples pass over opportunities that are offered in seminars, workshops, and presentations on child care, values orientation, or significant contemporary movements which affect family life.

The attitude of "doing it alone" deludes us into thinking that we are doing it right, and it eliminates the need for examining our effectiveness or facing our failures. The all too common query of "Where did we go wrong?" could be more effectively confronted by asking earlier, "How can we avoid these common mistakes of marriage and family life?"

Marriage and family enrichment should offer significant opportunities for growth and a better grasp of the meaning of our choices and promises (FC§72). However, there is sometimes a tendency for organizations to exist for their own sake, to grow inward, and to become esoteric. Those who have attended much publicized seminars, or those who have joined an organization having to do with marriage enrichment sometimes look upon those who haven't done so as lacking in something essential. There is a fine line of distinction between offering and encouraging growth and insisting that life is meaningless unless one has attended a particular seminar or joined a particular organization.

What is important is simple encouragement to all of us that we should seek ways of continuing and improving our awareness, that we should be open to learning, and that we should have the will power to apply what we are discovering. There is nothing automatic about the quality of family life. What happens there, as anywhere, results from specific effort and at the cost of personal energy.

WOMEN'S RIGHTS

From a pastoral point of view, we can rejoice that the document speaks of a broader role for women in the family and in the Church (FC§23). There is much which could be expressed here. It is a matter of history that women's roles have been grossly neglected by the Church as an institution. In most places women have been insensitively relegated to positions of secondary importance. Such expressions as "submission," "subjection," "honoring and obeying," "homemaking and caring for the needs of children," are overused and have effectively demeaned the position of women in the family. Only recently have we begun to speak of equality of roles and the special contributions which women have always made.

Any pastor will frankly admit that were it not for women, most activities and projects in the parish would go largely unattended. Concern for the religious socialization of children, preparation for sacraments, the teaching of prayers, and a sense of service to others are all principally undertaken by mothers. The insistence that men and fathers should assume their share of responsibility in these roles is just and reasonable. There is an almost universal notion that religion and religious sentiment should be left to women who until recently have been referred to as weaker and more emotional.

The Church, certainly priests and bishops, have their own work to perform in amending the stigma which has been imposed on women. Sexist language abounds in the Church and in pastoral expressions. It is gratifying that the document makes a specific effort to avoid the use of male-oriented language. Even so, thre are still headings which speak of "man" as generic and inclusive of women (FC§11). If this is the time for rethinking, it is also the time for bending more deeply to offer reconciliation.

In light of the document's contention that women are equal, with equal roles in the family, one can't help lamenting the stance of certain bishops and pastors who will not allow women to read in church at mass or be ministers of communion. There is no reflection here of the equality which should exist in the family of God. It is difficult to speak of the sanctity of the family while supporting discord within the family of the Church. The hope, of course, on the part of many is that a new and more open awareness can replace the old thinking that women are secondary in the family of the Church.

This more realistic thinking would obviously have good effects on marriage and the family. The old notion that women's roles are restricted to the home and children and to the lesser duties of the household, have at least implicitly been reaffirmed by the Church. A new awakening to the wider role of women and a more accurate appreciation of their contribution, offers women something of an apology for much neglect in the past. Obviously, this earnest approach will have a healthy effect on family life. It is easier for a person to assume and fill a given role with a more positive attitude when one knows one is needed and appreciated.

THEOLOGY

The custom of theology has been to voice some misgivings about what marriage is as opposed to celibacy and virginity. The intimation has ever been that marriage was at least in part a capitulation to the weaknesses of the fragile and suspect human body. Such giants as St. Augustine, St. Jerome, St. Gregory the Great, St. Bernardine of Sienna, to mention only a few, talked profusely in terms that denigrated sex and even marriage. And marriage, of course, was looked upon as inferior to celibacy.

No one today would maintain the rigid stance of these earlier theologians. But the residue of their thought still has its effect. Not too long ago one of the popes wrote an encyclical on virginity with a capital "V," and offered the notion that marriage was sacred, but virginity was a higher calling.

Familiaris Consortio makes an effort to correct the former thinking that marriage, sex, and the expression of sexual responses are somehow unholy submissions to the body. This represents a quantum leap forward and provides a new perspective (FC§11).

Scripture scholars continue to try to understand every expression of revelation. Much of their energy is directed toward clarifying the meaning of what Jesus says. What does it mean to sell what you have, give to the poor, and come follow him? What can Jesus be asking when he commands that if our eye is an occasion of sin to us, we should pluck it out and go through life blinded? How are we to respond to someone who tells us to live without material goods, no money, nothing but a walking staff?

Most theologians today would respond to these and similar questions by assuring their students that Jesus always spoke in ideals, what could and should be done. The ideal expressed might be that we should avoid sin at all costs, or that we have to be generous enough to share our goods with others, or that we have to develop a holy trust that when we do the work of the kingdom our life will somehow be in God's hands. Hardly anyone would hold that Jesus was speaking literally in such cases.

The task then becomes interpretation. What did Jesus mean when he spoke? The effort at interpretation does not always yield simple answers. There is no easy plan for the ominous difficulties with which life often confronts us. And the answers that do come to light sometimes raise further questions and need even more clarification. Scholars rightly tell us that some insights are still to be attained, are beyond our grasp just now, but may be discovered in the near future.

What did Jesus intend for marriage? Surely he spoke to an ideal; one partner for life, no re-marrying in the case of a premature end to one's current married relationship. Jesus gave these commands because divorce and separation even then were problematic; they caused the same kind of havoc and dislocation then in the lives of those affected by it as they do today.

Realistically, it happened then as now, that the ideal was not realized in all cases. But human limitations do not harm the ideal; they simply add to our conviction that circumstances, personal energy, background, the life we are given with its peculiar structure of care or neglect, and literally countless qualifications, all enhance or diminish our ability to personalize and realize ideals. Certainly this is true of marriage.

THE PROBLEM OF DIVORCE

Divorce is rampant in our time. Broken homes, splintered families, one parent relationships, and the ensuing pain which is so much a part of so many lives, all demand our attention and an effort at resolution. The ideal of marriage must be consistently upheld, offered to those who are marrying.

But Jesus was totally attractive to people because he listened, sympathized, and saw good where others found difficulty, as in his approach to the adulterous woman and to the landlord who extorted his clients. Jesus very rarely condemned; he saved his vitriolic salvos for hypocrites who refused to acknowledge their sins and lived the lives of whited sepulchres. At the slightest inkling of remorse, the least intimation of amendment, Jesus relinquished all judgments and concentrated on the good in people. Someone has recently said that the true basis of our relationship with Jesus is in our sinfulness. Jesus simply loved sinners. Most of us eminently qualify.

What then of the divorced, millions upon millions of individuals who have suffered the abysmal grief of disappointment and the stigma of what we have come to call failure? How do we treat them? What do we have to say? (FC§§83,84)

If Jesus' approach to sincere and contrite people is to be the criteria for our attitude toward others, then we must treat one another very well; no judgments as to sin, worthiness, or who is in favor. Once we acknowledge the lack of promise on the part of those who enter marriage too quickly, those who were arrogant and presumptuous, those who were too young and immature, there can be no recrimination, no living in what is past, if we are to be true Christians.

The meaning of family is that we must be ready to take anyone in. The deepest meaning of this concept should be clearly observable in the Church. Such meaning has little to do with laws about sacraments, judgments about which marriage is valid and which isn't, and denying the full benefits of family life from those who did not happen to succeed in a given area. Jesus came to call us all, and he might not have bothered if he had thought we did not need regrouping and acceptance.

Concluding Thoughts

Let me go back to my friend in the beginning. She is the kind of person we have come to designate as a deeply committed Christian. She entered marriage and Christian family life with studied conviction, a sense of service, and a willingness to make her contribution. My friend is a gifted person, more than ordinarily prepared to cope wtih life's constant demands. She had no control over the dissolution of her marriage. It has grieved her and created an incalculable loss.

What can *Familiaris Consortio* say to her? Does it speak only to healthy and untrammeled families? Certainly not. As all papal documents, it should be a voice of consolation to all who fall within the scope of its embrace, to all Christians.

It seems to me that the document is calling for a certain wholeness, for individual health, long before a person enters upon marriage and family life. There is little sense in gliding into a marriage with too many problems to solve, too much hidden agenda, with the expectation that marriage and the family will take care of it all.

Familiaris Consortio asks for a better developed, better prepared, saner person before marriage ever takes place. If the family is the seat of growth and nurture, it must offer these qualities in order to perpetuate and improve itself. There are no automatic or miraculous bursts of being here. Life is work, effort, and application. So are marriage and the family.

My friend will survive, continue to grow, and enter into new phases of life which will call forth from her responses that she might not have known were in her. The blessing of existence is so rich and filled with resources as to be virtually limitless. Hopefully, her family will always be in harmony with the lives of other families to make complete what was broken and abbreviated. That will happen because there is a wholeness which belongs to the community, to the gathered members of many families. That wholeness can only exist to a lesser degree in the individual and it looks to others for completion.

If the family continues to reveal its intrinsic good, it will be a result of its members' efforts to grow from within, individually and together. *Familiaris Consortio* is an expression of confidence that this is a clear possibility; it will be realized by those who are convinced that God's message to increase and fill the earth calls for the kind of fullness that makes room for, and accepts, every individual person.